The American Chronicles of José Martí

Reencounters with Colonialism:
New Perspectives on the Americas

editors

Mary C. Kelley, AMERICAN HISTORY, DARTMOUTH COLLEGE
Agnes Lugo-Ortiz, LATIN AMERICAN STUDIES, DARTMOUTH COLLEGE
Donald Pease, AMERICAN LITERATURE, DARTMOUTH COLLEGE
Ivy Schweitzer, AMERICAN LITERATURE, DARTMOUTH COLLEGE
Diana Taylor, LATIN AMERICAN AND LATINO STUDIES, NEW YORK
    UNIVERSITY

Frances R. Aparicio and Susana Chávez-Silverman, eds.
Tropicalizations: Transcultural Representations of Latinidad

Michelle Burnham
Captivity and Sentiment: Cultural Exchange in American Literature, 1682–1861

Colin G. Calloway, ed.
After King Philip's War: Presence and Persistence in Indian New England

Carla Gardina Pestana and Sharon V. Salinger
Inequality in Early America

Renée L. Bergland
The National Uncanny: Indian Ghosts and American Subjects

Susana Rotker
The American Chronicles of José Martí: Journalism and Modernity in Spanish America

Carlton Smith
Coyote Kills John Wayne: Postmodernism and Contemporary Fictions of the Transcultural Frontier

The American Chronicles of José Martí

Journalism and Modernity in Spanish America

Susana Rotker

Translated from the Spanish by Jennifer French
and Katherine Semler

University Press of New England
Hanover and London

University Press of New England, Hanover, NH 03755

Originally published in Spanish as *Fundación de una escritura: las crónicas de José Martí,*
by Editorial Casa de las Américas (Havana, 1992)

Printed in the United States of America

5 4 3 2 1

Library of Congress Cataloging-in-Publication Data
Rotker, Susana, 1954–
[Fundación de una escritura. English]
The American chronicles of José Martí: journalism and modernity in Spanish America
/ Susana Rotker ; translated from the Spanish by Jennifer French and Katherine Semler.
    p.   cm.—(Reencounters with colonialism—new perspectives on the Americas)
Includes bibliographical references (p. -) and index.
ISBN 0–87451–901–2 (cloth: alk. paper)—ISBN 0–87451–902–0 (pbk. : alk. paper)
1. Martí, José, 1853–1895—Criticism and interpretation. 2. Journalism and litera-
ture—Latin America. 3. Martí, José, 1853–1895 Escenas norteamericanas. 1. Title.
11. Series
PQ7389.M2 Z771313   2000
861—dc21   99–41912

With Love

To Sol-Ana, in her own language

To Tomás Eloy Martínez, who began it all

Contents

Preface   ix

Chapter 1. The Logic of Literary Representation   1

Chapter 2. The Writers' Role   15

Chapter 3. The Emergence of the Chronicle   31

Chapter 4. Writing the Present   60

Chapter 5. The Years in North America: Creating Local Lore
from Abroad   84

Chapter 6. Conclusion: Adventure and Transgression in Writing
and Reading   105

Notes   111

Index   137

Preface

Most books hold our interest briefly before they let us go; this one has held mine for years without ever loosening its grip. Perhaps this is because José Martí's writing turns out to be truly inexhaustible, forever suggesting and demanding new readings. Or perhaps the proximity of a new *fin de siècle* invites us to look closely at the previous century. Perhaps the chronicle as a literary and journalistic style has not yet found its due recognition despite the extraordinary production of chronicles in Spanish America on a daily basis. Perhaps the viewpoint of an exile in the United States challenges us to consider our own identity. All these themes are explored in this book; all have enveloped me, and I don't think they will ever truly let go.

The idea for this project began in 1983 at the University of Maryland while I was taking a course taught by Graciela Nemes. By pure chance, she assigned me an analysis of José Martí's chronicle on the death of Jesse James. That class presentation was expanded into a monograph, and then others, until it led to this project. The first stage lasted more than five years and included research in libraries, microfilm archives, and newspaper files in Washington, Caracas, and Buenos Aires. The second stage comes to an end now, sixteen years later.

I owe the idea of comparing the North American press, *La Opinión Nacional* of Caracas, and *La Nación* of Buenos Aires to Jorge Aguilar Mora. He also showed me that, in order to disentangle the complex literary web of a period, I needed to take into account trends of thought, history, and different modes of textual production. Part of my research was supported by a grant from the Social Science Research Council. I thank Joan Dassin, Francine Masiello, Beatriz Sarlo, and Josefina Ludmer for their help in defining a discursive genre between journalism and literature. Special mention goes to Doris Sommer who gave me not only generous theoretical suggestions from the outset but also the impetus to delve further into new perspectives on Martí's chronicles.

Thanks to José Emilio Pacheco for the rhetoric of the sublime; to Sylvia Molloy, María Luisa Bastos, Jean Franco, and Ana María Amar Sánchez for the materials they supplied; to Richard Morse for the discovery of Sousa Andrade's New York poems; to Marcos Pérez, Fernando DiGiovanni, Marcy Schwartz, and Jennifer French for corrections of the revised text; to Ilia Casanova and Jennifer Russo, who researched in the libraries to find quotations in their original English wording; to Margo Persin for her readings of my exilic reflections; to Roberto Fernández Retamar for his Martiesque faith; to Sergio Dahbar for sharing my interest in the "crónicas"; and to my parents for lugging books and papers from one end of the continent to the other for me.

I also thank Estela Lanari for inviting me to give a seminar on the chronicle at the University of Mar del Plata; Jaime Abello and Gabriel García Márquez for letting me confront my theories in a workshop at the Foundation for New Spanish American Journalism in Cartagena de Indias; the jury of the Casa de las Américas for the 1990 prize awarded to the Spanish edition of this book; my colleagues in the Department of Spanish and Portuguese at Rutgers University for their professional support; Donald Pease, Diana Taylor, and Agnes Lugo-Ortiz for believing that this book deserved translation; and Raúl Fernández, Jeffrey Belnap, and Julio Rodríguez-Luis for including recent fragments of my work on Martí in their editions *José Martí's "Our America": From National to Hemispheric Cultural Studies* (Durham: Duke University Press, 1998) and *Re-reading José Martí (1853–1895): One Hundred Years After* (Albany: State University of New York Press, 1999).

To my sweet Sol-Ana, who was born with this research project, and who, despite having lived since then with my obsessive presence in front of the computer and with many moves and readjustments, has managed to be the picture of solidarity and cheerfulness. To Tomás Eloy, generous companion and demanding reader, for "La segunda vida de Araya" (*El Nacional*, 1978) and his book *Lugar común la muerte*, which led me to discover that a moving form of literature had found a place in the daily pages of journalism long before my encounter with "Jesse James." His approach to literature and journalism has breathed life into this project from beginning to end.

The American Chronicles of José Martí

Chapter I

The Logic of Literary Representation

I. The Problem of Modernity

By 1888, the terms "modernism" and "modernity" were so intimately related for writers that Rubén Darío was using the two interchangeably.[1] At that time in Spanish America, modernity meant the perception of the beginning of industrialization and the consolidation of stronger bureaucratic states—only Cuba and Puerto Rico remained under Spanish hegemony—and the incorporation of that hemisphere into the international economic system.

To be modern meant, in general terms, a new atmosphere: railroads, steam engines, factories, telegraphs, daily newspapers, telephones, scientific discoveries, and urban centers that changed the shape of society and the distribution of traditional social classes. To be modern, in Western terms, meant faith in new technologies: man, as designer, would improve the material world and society would become a utopia thanks to his new efficiency. To be modern was, in the end, to subject oneself to the laws of the market, to adopt a transcontinental rather than regional outlook, and to face man's new condition as *animal laborans*[2]: a beast of burden.

According to Angel Rama, the relationship of modernism to modernity in Spanish America can be explained thus: "Modernism is but the conjunction of literary forms which explain the different ways in which Latin America was incorporated into modernity, a socio-cultural concept which was generated by the bourgeois industrial civilization of the nineteenth century."[3] This sociocultural concept, generated by the class whose interest it served, was betting that progress would bring a boundless future. According to this logic, if the contradictions in the lifestyles and the real conditions of Spanish America's heterogeneous population were exacerbated, the social costs incurred by growth would eventually be neutralized. José Martí explained:

As if to challenge reason, everything in nature that is logical appears to be contradictory. And so it happens that in this period of splendid expansion and transformation, despite all the obstacles to greatness, men prepare themselves to confront one another and be kings of kings. It is a time for poets, for great men. The confusion that the change of states, faith and government brings about makes this a time of upheaval and pain, in which the battle sounds drown out the melodious prophecies of good fortune for times to come. (VII, 224)[4]

Perceptions of change, of constant transformation and the mutability of space and knowledge, of the material gains of civilization, and even of the human organism itself simultaneously prevailed. It was an unstable system in which Darwinian ideas of evolution took root. Those who were most powerful were expected to triumph, and any evolution was seen as a change for the better.[5]

Although real industrialization became established in Spanish America only after 1920, the modernists submerged themselves in the *fin de siècle* maelstrom, thanks to the flow of information, the mixing of social classes, the possibility of travel, and violent urbanization.[6] In fact, the growth of large cities planned around powerful bureaucratic nuclei was such that, toward 1890, astonishingly, "the United States [was] less urbanized than at least four Spanish American countries: Venezuela, Chile, Uruguay, Argentina."[7] Furthermore, according to José Luis Romero's information, "nearly all the Latin American capitals doubled or tripled their population in the fifty years after 1880."[8]

These centers of great social mobility, most of them ports or coastal towns, continued to export raw materials and import manufactured goods. In fact, it was considered absurd to produce and more rational to uphold the logic of international specialization. The new bourgeoisie's mania for importation, according to Claudio Véliz, characterized what he calls "Latin America's liberal pause," which lasted about one hundred years from its beginnings in the mid-nineteenth century. Véliz affirms that the spirit of imitating all things European—a spirit that tends to be attributed to modernism—extended to the modes of consumption as well: "People were prepared to accept everything originating from France and Great Britain. They adopted their style of dressing, their architectural and literary fashions, their music, their manners, their affectations and exotic customs, and, almost unavoidably, their social, economic and political ideas" (177–78).

Transformed as were the hemisphere's great urban centers, there were still cities of great intellectual importance that continued to present a traditional aspect. For example, in his biography of Martí, Jorge Mañach describes Caracas as the Cuban knew it. "It displayed that peaceful, gentle feel that our cities get from their colonial tradition and from having economic sources outside the cities themselves; they retain something aristocratic and parasitic, as if they fed on the past and on peasantry."[9]

But the transformation that began in the large urban centers such as Mexico City and Buenos Aires[10] would soon spread, along with this contagious new spirit of modernity, to other Spanish American capitals. That peaceful, colonial feel became more and more scarce, as fewer and fewer citizens could remain immune to the international information that arrived with increasing regularity, not only through travel and books, but through journalism as well.

Modernity was, in its first instance, a system of *notions*: progress, cosmopolitanism, abundance, and an inexhaustible desire for novelty. All of these were derived from rapid technological advances, new systems of communication, and the logic of consumption which belonged to the laws of the new international market.[11] Nonetheless, neither the violent transformations that were beginning to introduce new privileges to the capitalistic lifestyle nor the apocalyptic sense of the imminence of the century's end can completely explain one concrete fact regarding the modernists: their intense malaise.[12]

2. Imbalance and the Coexistence of Heterogeneous Elements

There are numerous testimonies of imbalance in modernist poetry. They can be found in "Nihilism" by Julián del Casal: "Nothing of the future grabs my soul / and nothing of the present does it judge well at all; / if I look at the horizon, all is shadow, / if I lean toward the earth, all is ash." In "Las Almas Huérfanas" (The Orphaned Souls) by Gutiérrez Nájera: "man is dying of thirst, the orphaned souls are sobbing: Who brought us? Where did we come from? / Where is our home, our house?"

The poems of Rubén Darío also show signs of this obsession with "not knowing where we are going, nor from whence we came" as in "Lo fatal" (The fatal) from *Cantos de vida y esperanza* (Songs of life and hope). In Darío's work we find in addition the element of apathy: "Our parents were better than we are; they had a passion for something. The good bourgeois of the 1830s were worth a thousand times more than we are. Our own times flaunt the indifference of total moral stagnation; we don't think about anything with ardor. We aspire to no ideals with heart and soul."[13]

What had happened to projects of the future, to the power of feeling like the embodiment of the spirit of a new age? In 1887, José Martí proclaimed a new faith, with the enthusiasm of a Pierre Leroux, extolling those who gambled for freedom "in order that humanity one day might live a new life, the seed of which they harbored."[14] "It isn't about nursery rhymes or bedchamber aches, but rather the birth of an era, the dawn of the definitive religion and the rebirth of man . . . It is trying to reflect in words the sound of the settling multitudes, the laboring cities, the tamed seas and the enslaved rivers" (XIII, 140–41).

While one cannot completely conflate modernism with Martí, he too tempered his enthusiasm for modern man with a sense of disenchantment with urban life. This ambivalence is evident in his *Ismaelillo* or *Versos libres*, for example. If the modernists can be characterized by their desire to create spaces of condensation for contradictory elements—as in the symbol or the chronicle—the basic distinction between one and the others lay in Martí's formulation of a space of resolution for the contradictions of his time, for the paradox of disillusion and hope. For Martí the contradictions could only be resolved in the literary space of the struggle:

Not even the abundant study of the wondrous universal movement can satisfy us (among us it is cause for bitter jealousies and pain) *if it does not kindle within us the desire to do battle* . . . We do not have to see the other through the eyes of a child or the self through the eyes of an apostate. *Nor do we have to give in to this voice of fatigue and agony that comes from a spirit frightened by the din of mankind.* (VII, 20)

The malaise of Martí's contemporaries originated in the contradictions of rationalism, hope, the dislocation of man in the face of change, and the schism between nature and society. It originated, according to Angel Rama, in the economic displacement of modernists, the rapid increase in readership, the breakdown of long-standing cultural models, and the indistinctness of a new standard of values (Rama, "La dialéctica," 170 ff.).[15]

For Carlos Real de Azúa, "the new consciousness of integrating a social group with a more marked specificity than it had before—that is to say an *intelligentsia* . . . turned into malaise."[16] This malaise also involved the fact that governing bodies favored the modernists not because of their poetic work in and of itself, but rather because of their activities within official journalism, diplomacy, business, high bureaucracy, speech-writing, and other special services.

This was a period of drastic transition in lifestyles; inevitably, the push to preserve or impose models for each sector of society became more intense. The importing bourgeoisie urged a constructivist liberal discourse. The educated class—without opposing economic liberalism—forwarded a conservative discourse more anchored in the past and interested in adapting a national model. Land and ranch owners declared their ultramontane beliefs while new political strongmen supported populism. Peasant groups rebelled and organized ideologically around religious beliefs, while the urban proletariat of European immigrants grew more and more politicized.[17] In Cuba and Puerto Rico, in addition to the internal conflicts among economic sectors, were the issues of independence from Spain and the expansionist threat of the United States.

It was a conflict between old and new, between heterogeneous discourses framed by a cosmopolitan consciousness that accentuated contrasts. As Martí wrote in 1891: "We were a vision, a creature with the chest of an athlete, the hands of a dandy, and the forehead of a child. We were masqueraders, with English underwear, a Parisian vest, a North American jacket, and a Spanish mountain hat . . . We were chariots and togas in countries that came into the world wearing espadrilles on their feet and headbands on their heads" (VI, 20).

So there was more than one reality and more than one ideology. In terms of modernity as malaise, one can see the problem as almost tantamount to the existence of an elite whose singularity is a part of that very malaise. Although these divisions in Latin American societies were not absolute, we cannot ignore the fact that the modernists perceived themselves to be in a position similar to that of the nineteenth-century European writers: isolated between the uneducated classes and the bourgeoisie. Worse yet, although this classless position was very productive, many of the most critical modernist texts bear witness to their authors' frustration and guilt about serving the importing interests of the bourgeoisie, intermediary between internal power relations and world capitalism.[18] Modernism was about an intellectual elite that felt marginalized and alienated by the readjustment of social relations.

3. In the Crossroads: Man

Martí's chronicles offer one of the keys to deciphering the map of the power lines running through modernist sensibilities. His work goes beyond what is explicit in the aforementioned discourses: "Science increases man's ability to judge and feeds him with secure data, but in the end the problem will never be resolved. It will simply be better laid out. Man cannot be God, since he is man. We must admit how inscrutable the mystery is and do good, since this produces positive pleasure and lets man achieve some purification and growth."[19] The schism between science and the sense of inscrutable mystery was an epistemological dilemma, a crossing of various sensibilities and various modes of knowledge. Martí combined liberal faith in progress, reason, good deeds, and the perfectibility of man ("It is not enough just to be born: one must make oneself," he wrote in his notes [XXI, 40–41]) with Kantian discipline of will without reducing scientific method to utilitarianism as Auguste Comte had done. The above passage reflects Carl Christian Friedrich Krause's idea that beauty expresses good and truth, as well as the redemptionist bent of Saint-Simon and his disciples, who conceived of the poet as a priest in search of harmony.[20] However, he acknowledges that "the problem will never be resolved. It will simply be better laid out." This is a recurring theme of his: humanity is no longer the way it used to be and "knows not how it is," and the individual has not defined his rights, "knowing neither how, nor before whom he must vindicate them" (XXI, 226). This doubt is similar to that of Baudelaire, who, perplexed by the contradictions of rational, social, urban thought, asks, "Il court, il cherche. Que cherche-t-il?" and answers, "il cherche quelque chose qu'on nous permettra d'appeler la *modernité*."[21]

4. Rationalism and Romanticism

According to Max Weber, the process of modernization was in part propelled by the replacement of one system by another. The fixed and established parameters which traditionally structured human life were suddenly removed; the concept of destiny was deconsecrated as human society was reorganized around a new concept: "that there is, in essence, no mysterious and unpredictable force interfering and that, moreover, all things can be dominated by calculation."[22] Weber termed this process *rationalization*: the mastery of the material world, the systematization of all modes of life, the secularization of metaphysics.[23]

Although it is now common practice to apply Weber's concept to the nineteenth century, the certainty surrounding human control of space and nature began a few centuries earlier.

It is possible to trace secularization back to the Reformation and—needless to say—to the discovery of America, which changed the coordinates of Western knowledge dramatically. The idea of modernity is implicit in the very conception of America as the "New World."[24]

This demystification of the old transcendent order entailed a return to the idea that social reality is an order determined by mankind. The idea took root during the eighteenth-century European Enlightenment. In Spanish America, its greatest incarnation was perhaps the rationalizing spirit of post-independence writing, precisely during the stage that precedes modernism, if one can create a truly diachronic history of thought.[25]

Using Weber's ideas about modernization and rationalization, one could argue that Spanish American modernists were the writers of the post-independence period. For thinkers like Domingo F. Sarmiento, for example, writing was the way to consolidate widespread territories and diverse languages under a central authority: the void of discourse left by the antiquated colonial system needed to be filled. For Sarmiento, discourse was a means to civilize Latin America's wilderness. He wrote, "We, on the day after the revolution, needed to turn our eyes in all directions in an effort to fill the void that must have been left by the destroyed Inquisition, by vanquished absolute power, by widespread religious exclusion."[26]

In Martí and Darío's time, on the other hand, modernist writers suffered from displacement and vertigo. Familiar horizons were unstable and in perpetual flux. If we take into account the fact that Weber was theorizing from Europe at the dawn of this century—his texts were of the modernist vintage—and reconsider the period from a contemporary vantage point, we can no longer define modernity as simply rationalization. The reign of *method* and the will to systematize began to wane at the close of the nineteenth century, in the full climax of positivism. In Spanish America, this was the beginning of another period, that of the crumbling of certainty, the age of suspicion. The modernity that defined and identified its writers was a confrontation between rationalization and subjectivism, between the tedious routine of daily life and mythic consciousness, between disappointment and faith in the future. It was a desire to conceal the contradictions and fragmentation of reality, a desire for novelty and incessant change in a cosmopolitan environment.

The lives and discourses of the modernists took on a romantic guise in the midst of a technological age. They incorporated the aesthetic suggestions and modes of perception of Gautier, de Lisle, Hugo, Mendès, Wilde, Huysmans, and Poe, to cite just a few. They became a sort of echo chamber for all of Western culture, combining a search for all things personal and new with the truest of traditional elements.

It is useful to remember Octavio Paz's observation about the historical function of modernism as "similar to the [European] romantic reaction at the dawn of the nineteenth century [and that] their version was not a repetition but a metaphor: a different romanticism."[27] It was also a response to positivism and, further, to the utilitarianism that impregnated Spanish American schools with the ideas of Destutt de Tracy or Jeremy Bentham. Bentham's ideas were particularly convenient for the emerging bourgeoisie, based as they were on the principle of maximum pleasure for the maximum number of people as a moral and legislative criterion.[28]

Likening Spanish American modernism to European romanticism, as Paz proposes, discards rhetoric as a governing institution of literary production.[29] It has other cultural implications as well. In Europe, romanticism was a movement of social protest and religious, aesthetic, and moral politics. It took place during a period of such major revision of thought that we might, following Highet, call it a revolutionary period rather than a romantic one (Highet, 356).

As regards modernism and especially José Martí—the first to formulate the new poetics—Gutiérrez Girardot is sympathetic to the linking of modernism with romanticism if one considers these movements revolutionary. He says, drawing on Heidegger: "In this sense Martí was a 'revolutionary' . . . if by revolutionary we mean, not that 'the transformation' itself is what is essential, but that *with the transformation he illuminates that which is decisive, interprets it, ponders it, considers it*" (Gutiérrez Girardot, 78; emphasis added). This definition cannot be overlooked when considering the role of modernist poetics.

One decisive aspect of the *fin de siècle* was secularization. But it was an extreme secularization, for the process that had begun several centuries before became, at the end of Martí's century, the metaphor of the death or the absence of God. For those artists in search of romance as an antidote to the material vulgarization of everyday life, the absence of God also meant the end of time, the loss of a meaningful historical process in human history and its replacement by the mere certainty of progress.

This void was filled by modernists with a search for ontological beauty capable of reflecting the absolute, the infinite.[30] The fall of faith and the search for harmonic totalities were parallel, as were the need to look for immanence in the world and the sense that writers had no place within the new market-driven society. Caught between vulgar reality and the desire for eternity, the new man and "the dawning of the birth of a new era" did not exactly achieve the redeeming and "definitive religion" to which José Martí aspired. The new man was more akin to the amphibian in Hegel's *Aesthetics*: an amphibian forced to move among contradictions, after the demise of harmony.

5. Subjectivism, Historicity, and Legitimization

In the prologue to Pérez Bonalde's "Poema del Niágara," José Martí says that in his time: "a personal life full of doubt, alarm, question, anxiety, bellicosity; an intimate life full of fever, disturbance, vigor, and clamor has come to be the central issue and, along with nature, the only legitimate issue in modern poetry" (VII, 229). Since they no longer believed in a sacred tradition or an absolute law, men were left to organize their own coexistence. The experience of self-limitation for human beings is new, in historical terms, and even more so in Spanish America. In the late nineteenth century Spanish America remained heterogeneous, not totally independent from the Spanish metropolis, and in need of discovering its own identity. The horizons of the familiar world changed vertiginously under the banner of progress, making it necessary to search for general principles on which to found social order. All was subject to criticism.

Modernists believed that everything, somehow, had to move toward a final harmony. But the very concept of *everything* entered into the whirlpool of criticism. Modernists suffered—or began to perceive—an epistemological rupture: they no longer had before them "established maps that charted all the routes and paths . . . and knowledge itself, previously an indivisible relationship between the knowing subject and the object of knowledge,"[31] underwent an irreparable alteration. Foucault affirms that in the nineteenth century the Western episteme underwent a general redistribution, when he writes that "the knowledge of man should appear, in its scientific aims, as contemporaneous and of the same origin as biology, economics and philology" (345).

The epistemological debate that examined the privileges of science as well as the notion of historicity, also incorporated such claims as Hegel's that art had ceased to be the form in which truth manifested itself: these contemporary issues led the modernists to take a deeper interest in philology. In the effort to achieve both social legitimacy and reconciliation, they read and wrote about philology because it suggested working with language in a way that was not simple signification. Martí's comments suggest a combination of scientific rigor, historical profundity, and aesthetic sensibility: "Words have a layer that envelops them, that is usage: it is necessary to get down to their bodies. Something is broken in this examination, and depth is revealed. Words must be used as they are seen in this depth, with their real etymological and primitive signification, which is the only one that is robust, that assures that the idea it expresses will last" (XXI, 164). Philologists treated language in a way that was analogous to the work of biologists or archaeologists, which produced parameters consonant with the scientism then in vogue. Furthermore, philology was considered—as Renan pointed out—"the exact science of matters of the spirit. [Philology] is to the humanities what physics and chemistry are to the philosophical science of matter."[32]

Faced with the demise of everything permanent, the modernist writers found in philology a scientific method of approaching knowledge. Yet at the same time, they moved away from science because they rejected rationalism as being "a method to solve problems [that denies] the Universal applicability of all laws to all historical and social units."[33] They had to search for a new notion of truth in the intersection of contradictions and opposites, formulating a poetic system that could reconcile technique and emotion, the progress of material society and the need for transcendence.

This change in perspective overturned the system of representation: . . . given that at the same time the general theory of representation disappeared and, in turn, there arose the need to question the being of man as the fundament of all positivities, there could be no lack of imbalance: man became that from which all knowledge could be constituted before its immediate and nonproblematic evidence: *a fortiori*, became that which allows us to doubt all man's knowledge. (Foucault, 335)

This observation will be crucial to the analysis of modernist poetry. The "I" emerges as the only way to achieve authenticity, as Darío explained in "Dilucidaciones": "I have meditated on the subject of existence and have tried to reach the highest of identities. I have expressed what parts of my soul are expressible and I have tried to penetrate the souls of others and submerge myself in the vast universal soul . . . I've imbued the lyric instrument with my momentary will, but I am myself an organ of the instants, various and variable, subject to the whim of inexplicable fate."[34]

As in European romanticism, the new literature discarded the classical concept of art as an imitation of nature. Solipsism served both as a point of departure for artistic creation and as a way to obtain knowledge of the origins of life, since there was no universal law. The new literature had broken (or was breaking) with the classical system of representation: the modernists did not deal with *imitatio*. The "I" served also to organize the interwoven discourses of science, technology, philology, and literary and cosmopolitan erudition in the "organ of the instants." To the extreme individualism underscored during this period, the modernists responded by vindicating it as a method of hearing that which was true through that which was most authentic in the self.

Here, Martí also had his own slant. He claimed a creative subjectivity that was united with history: "Let us make our own history looking into our soul; and that of others looking at their deeds. There will always remain, over every upheaval, the subjective muse . . . and the historical one" (XXI, 226). Martí thus opened another "space of condensation," that is to say, a unique representation that links several associative chains, and resides at the point of intersection of those chains. The space opened here is that of the textual "I," neither romantic nor anonymous, as Fina García Marruz aptly observes, but rather a collective "I" that assumed man to be the "Universe unified. The universe is man in his variations" (XXI, 261).[35]

6. The Era of Suspicion

Affirming subjectivism as a source of authenticity seemed a contradiction in the age of technological fervor. The modernists incorporated into their language the awareness of philology as the "science of language." Either they had left off the imitation of Nature in favor of the modes of production, according to literary critic Noé Jitrik; or, in their search for a new harmony, they included at once ideas taken from Pythagoreanism, the occult, and Catholic iconography. They understood technique rather than inspiration to be the essence of writing, and practiced subjectivism as a mode of knowledge: the result was a method that surpassed the limits of science and connected subterraneously with currents of contemporary thought. Martí himself noted: "This is everywhere an epoch of reordering and remolding. The past century blew out, with an evil and forceful ire, the elements of the old life. Impeded by the ruins in its path, which threaten and excite with galvanic life at every moment, this century of detail and preparation accumulates lasting elements of the new life" (IX, 325).

The contradictions and disorder Martí describes here led to a system of representation that created new spaces of condensation, as we have seen and will discuss further. The past was clearly included in this excitement to construct a new life. Unlike the writers of the Independence era, who rejected their Spanish heritage in favor of the French and English traditions, Martí formulated his literary origin by mixing ideas and techniques from these cultures with elements recovered from the literature of Spain's Golden Age.

Another characteristic of the modernists' location between two stages of knowledge can be described as its *logic of literary representation*, the stock of culturally and historically determined assumptions upon which any linguistic description or characterization is based. The logic of literary representation is in fact any given epoch's epistemological system, the network of fundamental values and beliefs that condition and inform the production of knowledge at that time. The modes of production of a given culture, visible in the sensibilities of its literature, are intimately related to the logic of literary representation. In the case of the modernists, the logic of representation was based upon a willingness to question the dominant values of the nineteenth century: progress, positivism, and scientific objectivity. Certainly, the modernists shared modes of perception with Marx and Nietzsche, by whom the most fundamental assumptions of Western philosophy were brought into question. Their critical methods, together with the revaluation of the interior world of individuals, are the constitutive elements of twentieth-century thought.

Marx perceived an anxiety in facing the oncoming changes: "All fixed relationships, frozen rapidly, with their train of prejudices and old and venerable opinions, are swept away, all those that stop evolving become inadequate and they can ossify. All that is solid dissolves into air, all that is sacred is made profane, and in the end, men are forced to confront the real conditions of their lives and their relationships with their companions."[36] In playing with images this way, Marx gave a new character to the old interaction of opposites, perceiving that: "in such times everything seems pregnant with its opposite" (577).

Reality was ironic and contradictory. Man had constructed totalities in order to find his own context and meaning within them. The author ceased to be a spectator who reproduced reality by means of a universal concept. Instead he attempted to discover it through his own being, and, with Nietzsche, affirmed that "From the senses comes all credibility, all good conscience, all evidence of truth."[37] This attitude marks many modernist texts, whether or not Nietzsche directly influenced them.

The relationship between modernism and modernity cannot be taken for granted, since the term "modern" has had various meanings through the ages. As a matter of fact, Jürgen Habermas argues that the term came into use in order to distinguish the advent of the Christian era; he proposes that "modernity . . . has always expressed the consciousness of an epoch that understands itself in contrast to the past, as the result of a transition from old to new."[38] The modernists understood "modern" to identify a particular quality of those who were from a recent epoch, lived in the present, and, above all, saw themselves as making a transition into that which was new. Paz's definition helps us articulate their relationship with the twentieth century and locate the embryo of present dilemmas in the modernist malaise: "Modernity is a decision, a desire not to be like those who preceded us and a wish to be the beginning of another time" (*Poesía en movimiento*, 5).

The *fin de siècle* writers truly experienced a crisis between two epochs. Having discussed the results of rationalization, we will now turn to amplify and investigate more thoroughly the appearance of doubt or suspicion, which marked the commencement of another era.

In exploring the modernist chronicle as an element of transition into the present century, we can use the following parameters: the era of doubt—to give the contemporary scene a name—is defined neither by Weber's concept of rationalization nor by the hope that social progress and technology will bring about human happiness. Our disenchantment has to do with the loss of totalizing, teleological narratives and faith in the future; it is the breakdown of the image of unity; it is the heterogeneity and diversity of the processes of modernization. In the nineteenth century, the shared experience of science, morality, and modes of organizing social coexistence signified a tension that strained toward ultimate harmony; whereas in the twentieth century this energy is dispersed and diffused, the possibility of ultimate reconciliation is put in doubt. The modernity of our own era is more complicated than that described by Weber.[39]

Modernist texts expressed not only bedazzlement in the face of technology, but also a theme of estrangement, of being out of place and having no homeland, that would later be central to the theories of Freud and Heidegger. Here, as well, was the relativization of scientific knowledge that would lead Bertrand Russell to declare, "Mathematics is the science where no one ever knows what he is talking about or if what he is saying is true,"[40] and Roland Barthes to ask for a *mathesis singularis*, a science based entirely on subjectivity.[41] This is the epistemological schism that began with the Hegelian idea that the figure in which the truth exists can be nothing but the systematic elaboration of this truth. Today post-structuralists ask the question, "What is a scientific system?" and offer the response that *any* system is but another assertion.[42]

An epistemological rupture had begun, inaugurating "modern" knowledge as part of a "paradoxical unit," a unit of the disunity that "places us all within a maelstrom of perpetual disintegration and renewal, of battle and contradiction, of ambiguity and angst" (Berman, 15).

7. The Space of Condensation: The Symbol and the Chronicle

Martí observed that "we are in a time of agitation, not condensation; of a mixture of elements, of energetic workings of united elements."[43] The resolution of a new order will find its space in writing, as in all epochs of crisis. Laclau points out that the crisis "is translated into an exacerbation of all the ideological contradictions . . . This ideological crisis will translate necessarily into an 'identity crisis' of social agents. Each one of the agents in conflict will attempt to reconstruct an *ideological unit using a 'system of narration'* which dismantles the ideological discourse of opposing forces."[44] According to Laclau, one of the possible solutions to the crisis is that a social faction may develop an interpellation with all of its implications and transform it as much into a criticism of the existing system as a principle for restructuring the entire ideological domain.[45]

Therefore, we must analyze how modernists formulated their "system of narration," the way in which they arrived at unity after the rupture. We have mentioned thus far epistemological cracks, antagonistic intersections, crises, dialectics, and synthetic systems of narration. The synthesis lies in the idea of the space of condensation.

Associative chains were formed from the devices of symbol and analogy. Modernist prose and poetry, not unlike the work of the French symbolists, derived a system of symbology inspired by the eighteenth century philosopher Emmanuel Swedenborg and his theory of *correspondences*: "If man were involved in the knowledge of correspondences, then, he would understand the Word in its spiritual meaning. In this way it would be granted him to understand arcana of which he sees no trace in the literal meaning. The Word does contain a literal meaning and a spiritual meaning."[46]

This conception of the word was similar among symbolists and modernists.[47] Symbolists like Baudelaire thought of synesthesia not as the contact between interior vision and the divine, but rather as the connection between the mind and the senses. In the texts, the word took on a power akin to that of music. It provoked, by stimulating one of the senses, a multisensory plane of images. Poetry would acquire the flexibility to create, through the description of a sensation, the very sensation itself.

This ambition was the point of departure for modernist syncretism, which incorporated into literary expression procedures and techniques that pertained not only to music, but also to painting and sculpture. Martí maintained that "the writer must paint like the painter" (XX, 32). Gutiérrez Nájera looked "to form with words a bad canvas from the Rembrandt school, to oppose light with shade, intense black with brilliant white."[48]

Poets incorporated a multiplicity of artistic techniques and tendencies into their work, striving to develop a poetics that would reflect the present in all its variability. Modernist texts registered cosmopolitanism, anti-economist idealism, elitism and social compassion, religiosity, hispanism and francophilia, Latin Americanist and anti-yankee sentiment, the cult of popular heroes, and more. Along with symbolist techniques were mixed impressionism and even naturalism. The result was an assortment that transformed literary discourse and created a space of synthesis.[49]

Rubén Darío's description of the symbol in "Coloquio de los centauros" is a perfect way to define the space of condensation: "as in the wisdom of Nature, the symbol joins together *diverse forms.*" It was in the process of uniting diverse elements that modernists attempted—not always successfully—to embrace duality as a system and to employ writing as a point of encounter between such antagonistic pairs as spirit/matter, literature/journalism, prose/poetry, old/new, foreign/domestic, "I"/collective, art/systems of production, nature/artifice, man/animal, conformity/resistance.

Martí himself supported this thesis concerning spaces of condensation, although in different terms. He considered his epoch to be analytical or critical—dispersing its elements in a dialectic way—as opposed to epochs of faith, which were "capricious syntheses" (XII, 199). The space of condensation should be understood not as a synthesis, but rather as a dialectic encounter, neither static nor resolved, where "diverse forms come together." For Martí, the movement from criticism to synthesis was successive, aspiring to a final synthesis: his idea was, coincidentally, explainable in terms similar to Marx's because "the perfect genius is the one who with the supreme power of moderation explains both analysis and synthesis without disregarding one in favor of the other or denying one because of the other, and rises to the synthesis by means of analysis" (XII, 236).

Just as the image of the centaur was the prototype of the man/animal duality, the chronicle took form in a space of condensation par excellence. It is a modernist condensation because it encompassed all mixtures, as it was a mixture itself converted into a singular and autonomous unity.

Chapter 2

The Writers' Role

1. The City

The modernists' environment was the city. Surrounded by aristocratic provinces still smelling of the colonial past, urban centers grew as bureaucratic hubs where traditional authority led a system of sinecures and prerogatives. Civil, commercial, and legal power was enforced from urban capitals long before industrialization had been tangibly consolidated.[1]

Some Spanish American cities grew at such a rate that, by 1890, Mexico City had almost as many inhabitants as Rome (close to four hundred thousand) and Buenos Aires boasted more than half a million. New York, meanwhile, reached a million and was the foremost industrial and commercial center of the time (Romero, 250–59). Claudio Véliz explains the disproportionate figures thus: "It is evident that the inhabitants of these urban centers were neither farmers nor peasants, nor were they industrial workers . . . : they served one another, were employed by the service or tertiary sector of the economy, which included domestic services as well as teachers, lawyers, dentists, government employees, commercial dependents, politicians, soldiers, doormen, accountants, and cooks."[2]

The development of the urban service economy had its roots in the tension between urban groups and traditional social sectors, a conflict that lasted through much of the nineteenth century. The oligarchy, connected to huge provincial estates known as *latifundios*, limited "urban growth, national integration, and the creation of a modern bourgeois state."[3] It also limited land control, which is why urban groups in the eighties opened themselves up to the international sphere and specialized in mercantile commercial activities, finances, and the promotion of new goods and services.

In Spanish America urbanization advanced according to international commerce. At the apogee of industrialization, Europe and the United States established direct control over the countries in which raw materials abounded, spurred by the accumulation of capital, the necessities of unchecked urban growth, and manufacturing's constant need for materials. These foreigners transformed Spanish America's economic structure by investing capital and employing a national workforce to install enterprises whose objective was not to develop, but rather to extract. Latin America's capital cities were redesigned and filled with foreign banks: "the cities that were becoming wealthier did not yearn for [the] peace [of provincial life] but for the whirlwind of activity that engendered wealth and could be turned into ostensible luxury" (Romero, 247–49). The resulting demographic and economic concentration broke the traditional balance between urban and rural power, and cities took on a greater role in political decisions and government administration. Furthermore, as Marcos Kaplan has explained, "The balance between the State, located in the capital, and the interior provinces [was] broken. Metropolitan centers absorbed wealth, population, power . . . and all this reinforced resentment and all kinds of conflicts" (187).

The city dictated a new social pyramid in which—besides the landed oligarchy—the dominant class included economic, political, military, and religious leaders. The intermediary layers comprised bureaucratic groups, the military, liberal professionals, and small and medium-sized industrialists. Immigrants, in some of the countries, gradually added to this layer.

As a category, the "learned" of the colonial era moved toward extinction, as politicians began to take over State discourse. Writers had to make a new place for literature in a society where the value of exchange in the marketplace and the notion of usefulness were primary.

2. The Redefinition of Discourses

In Europe, the process by which writers were separated from the social mainstream began in the renaissance, when authors first began to produce writing for a free market. This distinction became exaggerated during the romantic period when writers displaced from political power began to take their identity from that very displacement. They did this with the attitude of priests of art, aestheticizing private life and labor in the same problematic system of representation. An aristocracy of intelligence came into being, "a charismatic representation of the production and reception of symbolic works"[4]; a new social space was established for this privileged minority of authors and readers.

On the separation between State and literary discourses, Jürgen Habermas explained that the bourgeois model strictly divided what pertained to the private sphere from what pertained to the public. A third sphere of politicians and bureaucrats was established to mediate between the necessities of society and those of the State; this sphere would not permit "the mediation of other private persons in its political use of reason."[5] Writers as well as journalists therefore became part of the market of cultural goods. For Habermas—whose observations refer to nineteenth-century Europe—power, in the form of the State, stood sharply divided from the community of citizens. The literati therefore established themselves in the space between the private sphere and the state—in the public spaces of cafés and salons.

Around the same time period in Spanish America, the public sphere exhibited similar habits. But in José Luis Romero's view, which is fundamental to understanding the role that the modernist writer will later assume, the discourses were not separate. "The literato-journalist was a spokesperson of the small community whom everyone knew and from whom everyone expected arguments and glosses in favor of or against the palpitating question of the day" (Romero 246).

When the beginning of the violent urbanization of this hemisphere initiated the separation of political and literary discourses, the heirs to the society of humanist aristocrats were forced to search for a discourse of their own and break ties—as Habermas would say—with the declining public sphere of the *court*.

3. Literature as Vocation in Spanish America

Habermas's theory is useful for understanding *fin de siècle* literature, but some distinctions are needed to locate the social function of the modernist chronicle. First, the theory of the separation of the State with its vigilant role and the legitimization of a social action at the economic level through an ideology of exchange applies only to England during a brief period of the nineteenth century.[6] Furthermore, Habermas fails to note that the true nature of political life reveals the participation of different forces in constant rearticulation. The limits of official institutions are a prime example: other forms of social interaction, such as technology, diverse symbolic practices, and other institutions contributed to the definition of values (national security, benefits, growth).

If we adapt Habermas's categories to the specific conditions of time and place, we see that what began in Spanish America at the end of the nineteenth century was a tendency toward specialized discourses, as also indicated by Kaplan, Véliz, and Romero. Pedro Henríquez Ureña affirms that *fin de siècle* society saw "a division of labor. Men of intellectual professions tried to remain close to the task they had chosen and abandoned politics . . . And since *literature was not* really *a profession but a vocation*, men of letters became journalists or teachers if not both."[7] It is important to see here the discursive separation of profession and vocation in relation to literature. These notions were decisive in constructing an aesthetic and the source of more than one faulty interpretation of the characteristics of modernism.[8]

Another point worth highlighting, which moves away from Habermas's scheme, is that, in Spanish America, discursive differentiation did not mean that writers abandoned political themes. We have concrete examples in the texts of Darío, José Asunción Silva, Manuel Díaz Rodríguez, Juan José Tablada, José Santos Chocano, Leopoldo Lugones, Guillermo Valencia, and Julio

Herrera y Reissig. Many modernists participated fully in politics, from José Enrique Rodó and Baldomero Sanín Cano to José Ingenieros and Alcides Arguedas, to name a few.

The difference for turn-of-the-century writers and militant authors such as Martí and González Prada was that literature, as such, became disconnected from what Habermas calls the "publicity" for the judicial/political superstructure or *res publica*. Instead, literature was there "to take care of the common good . . . [through] a public representation of power."[9] Writing was becoming a practice opposed to the discourse of the State. Even so, many modernist essays maintained the political authority of literary representation; a good example of this is José Martí's "Nuestra América." Other texts that supported State discourse turned out to be effective more in the realm of prestige than of real power.

In a letter to a fellow writer, Rodó clarifies the panorama of specializations and his commitment to literature as a vocation: "Perhaps you are not unaware of this tragedy in South American life that pushes anybody with a pen in his hand toward politics. And I don't consider this to be an altogether bad thing. It all depends upon not allowing ourselves to be stripped of our personality."[10] He thus describes as "tragic" the paradoxical character of South American literary culture, in which the purity or disinteredness of writing is valued and yet where "anybody with a pen in his hand" is called to participate in politics. Rodó's final warning is most important: political engagement threatens to strip the writer of his "personality," and he must defend his creative autonomy in the moment of writing literature.[11]

Despite the evidence of professional specialization, the modernists had a whole range of occupations. Martí was a journalist, lawyer, teacher, storyteller, translator, orator, political activist, editor, consul to Argentina and Uruguay, and university professor of philosophy, literature, and law. Darío was a grammar professor, librarian, customs agent, journalist and foreign correspondent, private secreary to the Nicaraguan presidency, and consul to Colombia. Del Casal was a bureaucrat, journalist, and student of literature. Silva was a diplomat and businessman. Belonging to the educated classes was still useful in the job market and helped the modernists to obtain their many positions. The writers saw these posts as mere obligations, marginal to their careers but necessary to their economic survival. As Rama explains, "What the poet abandoned was the multiplicity of functions that had justified and explained, beyond the possible artistic excellence of his works, his place in social life and his historical role in a given traditional community."[12]

Poetry did occupy a place of its own, especially as separate from commerce. For the modernists, therefore, what was profitable and what was poetic were separate. When they were forced to define a purely literary sphere, they found that the category of the aesthetic was essential to them.

4. Morality, Redemption, and Beauty

Urban society revolved around money and practicality. Contemptible times, Martí called them, because "there is no primary art other than filling the pantries of houses, sitting in a golden chair and living a golden life" (VII, 223). Contemporary critics judged art in relation to the decadence of the times; in 1870 Eduardo Wilde wrote that art was "a malady of the intelligence, an abnormal state of mind that has the usefulness of luxury."[13] Literature was also understood as an object of leisure and pleasure, a luxury for the cultured elite.

But art was to carry out a social function of another kind. Since literature was no longer a necessary vehicle for national rationalization, its new role was that of a moralizing instrument. It used beauty to counteract—through education, for example—the materialism, emptiness, and amorality that capitalistic life styles brought about. Martín García Merou wrote that the so-called cult of letters was a way to save souls "who, without a temple to face the battle, give themselves up like courtesans to their seducers' caresses."[14] There was already the feeling that the modern man, having become an *animal laborans*, had been stripped of something. Habermas developed the concept of "residual need" to refer to the unfulfilled desires that were suppressed by the systems of needs implanted by the new philosophies of scientism and strategic-utilitarian morals. Art, if we discount its commercial market value, functioned as a vehicle to re-endow society with noble or transcendent feelings. It provided positive values that were otherwise displaced by quotidien routine: naturalness, spontaneity, and altruism. Art was supposed to "elevate thoughts, ennoble the spirit . . . [defend] the victims of bourgeois rationalization."[15] José Martí wrote:

What ignorant person maintains that poetry is not indispensable to societies? There are people so short-sighted that they cannot see the fruit for its rind. Poetry, whether it unites or separates, strengthens or distresses, supports or knocks down souls; whether it gives or destroys faith and courage, is more essential to the population than industry, since the latter only provides a means of subsistence, while poetry gives people the desire and the strength for life. (XIII, 135)

For Martí, art was not a means of escaping from life's worries, but rather a way to infect the population with a desire for knowledge and transcendental searches. For José Enrique Rodó, "a sense of beauty, a clear vision of what is lovely in life, leads to a broad and noble understanding of life."[16] Unlike Martí, however, the author of *Ariel* felt that an aesthetic sensibility and the love of beauty have "enough value to be cultivated for their own sake."

For the modernists, the social function of art was to elevate the spirit and the mind by sheltering them from the alienating effects of routinized labor, preserving nonmaterial pleasures, and providing images and ideals as compensation and motivation. Modernist writers agreed on this principle of separating themselves from commercialization and monetarism. They coincided with the romantic German belief that the artist was like the priest of an interior temple dedicated to the values of art and beauty.[17] In their search for purity, they approached a form of beauty "uncontaminated" by reality. As José Asunción Silva wrote: "They call *reality* all that is mediocre, trivial, insignificant, despicable . . . Reality! Real life! Practical men! . . . Horrors! . . . To be practical is to commit to a nasty and ridiculous enterprise."[18]

Spanish American modernists were familiar with the works of art being produced in Europe at the time. There, poetry was ruled by a quasi-religious Parnassianism that concentrated on composition and poetic style as a higher form of truth. Theories of the autonomy of language occupied symbolists like Baudelaire, Mallarmé, and Valéry, all of whom influenced modernist texts. Their imaginative cosmos was fed by the Kantian belief in the universality of the sublime and the fusion of the three concepts of truth, beauty, and goodness. These theories were simultaneously postulated by both Spanish Krausianism and the New England Transcendentalists, especially Ralph Waldo Emerson.[19]

New communication technology and the increased ease of international travel kept Spanish American modernists well informed about new, cosmopolitan developments in literature and culture, and they too began to propose the autonomy of literary discourse. They did not go to the extreme of many of the Europeans, however. (Flaubert, for example, had wished to write a book "about nothing," absolutely disconnected from exterior reality but made meaningful by the interior force of its style.)[20] In fact, we must not forget that the exquisite protagonist of José Asunción Silva's *De Sobremesa*, who repudiated with horror anything practical, was also a prosperous businessman with political and economic plans for national development. Darío himself came to renounce his isolation in *Cantos de vida y esperanza*: "tempted by ivory towers, / I tried to hole up in my mind / and hungered for space and for air / from the deep shadows of despair" (Darío, 245).

Martí always denied the empty formalism of the "art for art's sake" movement. For him, the writer had a clear social mission: "He must use his poetry as a whip, to punish those who try to take away human freedom, or who steal money from the people with their clever laws, or who want their countrymen to obey them like sheep and lick their hands like dogs. Poetry should not express whether one is happy or sad, rather it should be useful to the world and show that nature is beautiful" (XVIII, 349).

Martí's militant insistence on moral value did not mean that he renounced or neglected the pursuit of aesthetics and form. It was obvious to him that "language had to be mathematical, geometric, and sculptural. The idea must fit exactly into the sentence, so exactly that it is impossible to take anything out of the sentence without subtracting the same element from the idea as well"

(XXI, 225). Every feeling should have its own color, every thought its precise wording, so that "every emotion has its feet . . . Willows should be painted with light verse, sort of slender, and the trunk of an oak with rough, twisted, and profound words."[21] One of the traits that qualifies Martí as a modernist poet was what José Antonio Portuondo called "the modernist will to style."[22] This insistence on formal precision converged with the idea that the sublime is the essence of life.

Thus, in the case of Spanish America, "pure art" and the admiration of form should not be interpreted as a love for aesthetic theory as the highest form of wisdom, but rather as an emphasis on the autonomy of poetic language. By the phrase "autonomy of poetic language" we refer to the text's ability to elicit reponses from its audience: the perception of beauty, the pure contemplation of the text free from worldly distractions, and finally an appreciation of its skillful and inspired construction.

"I am after a form," said Darío. The modernists believed in poetic form as an instrument of revelation, an important distinction from the pursuit of art for art's sake. For the modernists, the contemplation of beauty taught one to appreciate and care for the cosmic totality, instilling a sort of profane religiosity and dedication into what Darío called the "rhythm of the immense celestial mechanism." In *Prosas profanas* Darío explains the common modernist belief in a harmonic law that explains the world not as "a series of acts, separated by catastrophes," but rather as a single, immense act elaborated by an incessant labor of union.[23]

Rejecting the utilitarianism of the time, modernists approached society, culture, and verbal nuances with a different sensibility. They struggled to recover the harmony and meaning that had been lost from cultural discourse. Gutiérrez Nájera wrote, "Beauty is necessarily ontological: it is absolute, it is God." If beauty was God, then the writer was its priest: "God reveals himself in the sublime creations of poets . . . Using a mathematical formula, we could say that beauty is to the artist what perfection is to a saint."[24]

Thus "verse is the sacred cup," as José Asunción Silva wrote. The profane poet grazed the realm of the divine, as Darío suggests in his "Responso" to Verlaine. As followers of Fourier and Saint-Simon, the modernists positioned themselves outside of commercialism, representing themselves as prophets of the future, critical of the vices of bourgeois society and inclined toward the achievement of ultimate plenitude. They often referred to the present but dissociated themselves from the recent past; they enriched the visual imagination with their affinity for nature and references to mythology, all scrutinized by their own ambivalences as Catholics in the era of secularization and cosmopolitanism (Gullón, 165–67).

This was not vacuous art or art without direction. Rather it was a precursor, a pelagian breath. Bent on harmonizing the contradictions of the time, they resorted to the symbol, which, "As Nature knew, joins disparate elements."[25]

Their identification with the ideals of good and beauty led modernists to create works of luxury and splendor. They treated language like a gem and their interior world like a kingdom. Rubén Darío wrote the following in his "Coloquio de los centauros" (in *Prosas profanas*): "The cries of three hundred geese will not keep you, woodsman, from playing your charming flute, as long as your friend the nightingale is pleased with your melody. When he is no longer there to hear you, close your eyes and play for the inhabitants of your interior kingdom" (Darío, 181).

The modernists felt themselves so far removed from the "three hundred geese" of the bourgeoisie that they chose to represent themselves as characters in their narratives. The result was a group of European-style novels, including José Martí's *Amistad funesta* (1885), José Asunción Silva's *De Sobremesa* (1887–1896), Manuel Díaz Rodríguez's *Idolos rotos* (1901), and Rubén Darío's stories "El rey burgués" and "El reino de la reina Mab" from *Azul* (1888).

5. Ambivalence and Contradiction

Rubén Darío cites Leonardo DaVinci: "And if you are all alone, you are all your own." The writer's voice constructs within the text a private place of representation, a refuge and above all a reserve in which to seclude himself. Yet he clamors simultaneously, to open himself up to cosmic comprehension.[26]

This contradiction between representing the private and the cosmic was one of the riddles that most fascinated the modernists. Complicating matters further, the space the poets reserved for themselves coincided with the bourgeois *interieur* they so clearly despised. As Walter Benjamin describes it, "The bourgeois who squares his account with reality in his office demands that the interior be maintained in his illusions . . . For the private individual, the private environment represents the universe. In it he gathers remote places and the past. His drawing room is a box in the world theater."[27] In this way the modernists, searching for the sublime and uncontaminated, tended to reproduce bourgeois habits: they sought distraction from reality and the re-creation of the universe in their individual fantasy.[28] Although modernists were opposed to the new capitalistic values, they seemed to express themselves, metaphorically, with the same cultural goods the economic elite imported from Europe to adorn their homes and their bodies: refinement, fashion, luxurious and exotic images, accumulation.

To these preferences the modernists added their disdain for vulgarity, expressed through a refinement of the senses. This combination of characteristics was easily misunderstood as akin to the ostentatious and superficial aristocratic inclinations of the bourgeoisie they so despised.

This is one of the contradictions that appears in their writing. As we saw in the previous chapter, the entire period was characterized by instability, transition, and the sensation that everything was pregnant with its opposite. The transition from a rural society to an urban one also implied a dialectic between degraded traditional lifeways and the emergence of the modern, conflictive and unstable as it was. Modernists occupied a social position that was structurally contradictory. Whether through family, lifestyle, or access to knowledge, they belonged to the dominant educated class, but they did not have a secure place in the mining, farming, or industrial oligarchy, nor at the top of the urban social pyramid led by commerce, the Church, and the military. *Fin de siècle* writers belonged neither to the oligarchy nor to the popular classes. Their lack of definition was typical also of the new urban middle tier, in which they were often included (Bourdieu, 22–23). But they were also instruments, helping to legitimize the dominant class through the dissemination of ideology in cultural discourse. The worldview of the majority of the population was shaped by ideas gathered from education, the press, and art: in other words, from the work of the intelligentsia (Kaplan, 196).

We have said that the modernist idealization of art developed from a critique of contemporary culture; however it cannot be denied that much of their work in fact supported the dominant classes. As Calixto Oyuela, one of the most renowned critics of the time, wrote, "nothing requires a greater elevation of the spirit or a more exquisite refinement than the contemplation and enjoyment of beauty."[29] If "exquisite refinement" was a requirement for understanding the beautiful, then the world of art and aesthetics was necessarily inaccessible to the uneducated laboring classes, and having access to culture therefore meant belonging to a certain elite.

The modernists were disgusted to see themselves as producers of commodities, identified against their will with the values of Darío's "rey burgués" (bourgeois king). However, this rejection of the bourgeoisie did not imply that they were writing for the masses: if it were not for their chronicles, inserted into the public space of daily news, the modernists would have reached only the most culturally sophisticated elite.

Bourgeois society recognized the moralizing function of art in principle, but in reality poetry occupied a miniscule and marginal space in Spanish American culture. Many writers complained about the difficulty of finding someone willing to publish their work, and about the very limited editions that were generally produced. In his *Autobiografía*, Darío remembered his experience in Buenos Aires: "When I lived there, publishing a book was a tremendous feat, only possible for someone like Anchorena, or Alvear, or Santamarina. It was like buying an automobile now, or a race horse . . . Editors? Not a one."[30]

Modernist poets were clearly excluded from the book industry. Even a writer as supported in official spheres as Leopoldo Lugones did not have much public response to his publications. The thousand copies of *La guerra gaucha* must have been bought by the Minstry of War, the Ministry of Public Instruction, and the Education Council.

The slow sales of modernist poetry cannot be attributed to a lack of readership, since more realistic or representational works sold well in Spanish American markets. Miguel Cané sold out of a thousand copies of *Juvenilia* in just a few days; a novel by Eugenio Cambaceres sold two thousand copies in a week. In 1902, Eduardo Gutiérrez's *Juan Moreira* "had surpassed the famous sixty-two thousand copies of *Martín Fierro*" by José Hernández (Prieto, 50–51).

Sales figures are significant not only because they are an index of the fickle market. What is interesting is that they locate modernism with respect to other modalities of writing and social engagement that were as important at the time as they have become in literary history. Movements and genres such as naturalism, realism, *criollismo*, and historical fiction produced turn-of-the-century bestsellers of literary quality and social commitment.

In order to understand better the significance of modernist poetics, we must see this work in its contemporary cultural context, which was not only that of European trends, as some literary historians have insisted. We must also consider the panorama of contemporary literary production in Spanish America, much of which was marked by a radically different understanding of literary form and function. While modernist writers were generally excluded from the book market, a substantial group of important works was being published, including works that showed their authors' indifference to modernism's aesthetic innovations and independence of traditional mimesis. It was the novels of manners, along with realist and naturalist texts, that were attracting readers and achieving commercial success, works as different from the modernists' as Clorinda Matto de Turner's *Aves sin nido*, a novel about the displacement of indigenous peoples in Peru. Other examples include Javier de Viana's *Gaucho*, Manuel Payno's *Los bandidos de Río Frío*, Ignacio Manuel Altamirano's *El Zarco*, Lucio Vicente López's *La aldea grande*, José López Portillo's *La parcela*, Federico Gamboa's *Santa*, Eugenio Cambaceres's *En la sangre* and *Sin rumbo*, Carlos Reyes's *Beba*, and *La charca* by Manuel Zeno Gandía. These contemporaneous works represented a diversity of relationships to society and a wide range of aesthetics and ideologies—positions that are doubtless also tacitly present in modernist writing, which was, like all literature, a critical response to both literary tradition and the social status quo.[31]

6. Against Mental Cliché

Modernist poets introduced a new system of representation into the social imaginary, a palette of cosmopolitan and sophisticated sensory images that conveniently coincided with the lifestyle then developing in the cities. Françoise Perús has advanced this thesis, suggesting even that the modernists' poetics resembled bourgeois economics. According to Perús, the modernists' assimilation of European influences affirmed their independence from Spain but created a new form of dependence (Perús, 64 f.).[32]

Juan Marinello maintains, on the other hand, that although it did produce a genuinely Spanish American voice, modernism was "the dazzling vehicle of a shameful evasion, the brilliant miner of a naked fault."[33] "What for a European writer meant a critique of science and industry from his position of exclusion in capitalist society, to the Latin American was an affirmation of the special position of the artist."[34]

Angel Rama inverted the terms of these definitions when he gave a positive sense to the "universalization" that modernists brought to literature. He said: "Modernism served the people inasmuch as it understood the need to appropriate the instruments, that is, the rules and literary devices of literature created with the help of the European economic universe" (*Rubén Darío y el modernismo*, 124–25).

This interpretation is probably the closest to the modernist ideal. Nevertheless, the topic was central at the time, and there were quite a few personalities who denied Spanish Americans any creative capabilities. In Argentina, Juan Bautista Alberdi, who believed in the need to import literature and to adapt it to Spanish American tastes, said, "In a place where we don't make cloth, satin, velvet, Breton lace, burlap, crystal, porcelain, mirrors, statues, engravings, etc., how can we make heavy books written and published the way they appear in the most cultured parts of Europe?" (quoted in Rivera, 40). José Martí also remarked the precariousness of local culture: "For Literature we have practice drills and mewlings, we have the raw materials to create it, stray notes that are vibrant and powerful, but we don't have Literature itself. Our letters will not be expression until we have an essence to express with them. There won't be Spanish American literature until there is Spanish America (XXI, 163–64)."[35]

There is, however, a substantial difference between Alberdi and Martí: for modernists, appropriating and modifying was neither the goal of their literary project nor a solution to literary orphanage. According to Martí, culture warranted consideration regardless of its place of origin, as long as it did not merely imitate foreign tradition or reject its own. He asked: "Don't those who limit themselves to copying the spirit of foreign poets see that in doing so they admit that they have no nation, no spirit of their own, that they are nothing but shadows of themselves, walking the earth supported only by charity?"[36] The modernists steered toward internationalism, toward an attempt to integrate Western cultural discourse into the new urban reality of Spanish America. They strove for a future in which these "rudimentary countries" would be able to have a more modern culture.

Both the modernists' image of the world and the luxury of their poetics were connected to the issue of progress, the dazzling new frontiers of knowledge, the culture of industrialized countries, and the practical capabilities of man. Furthermore, modernists reflected the pain of transformation, and a frustrated desire to regain a feeling for the sublime and to create new spaces of condensation in a world where everything seemed fragmented.

Much of their writing was confessional, marked by a touch of the Baudelairean dandy as in these lines by Casal: "I love only wretched beings. The happy people who are satisfied with their lives drain me, they sadden and morally disgust me. I abominate them with all my soul."[37]

Modernism varied according to the author and the period. Max Henríquez Ureña commented usefully on the multiple roles of modernist literature:

In the second phase an inverse process unfolded [inverse to the "preciosity" of early modernism]; here personal lyricism reaches its most intense manifestations before the eternal mystery of life and death, while at the same time the anxious desire to achieve a genuinely American artistic expression predominates. Capturing the life and ambience of the people of America, translating their worries, ideals, and hopes, these were the goals of modernism in its final stage, without ever abdicating its first premise of working the language with art.[38]

There were individual differences and different periods within modernism. How, then, to ascertain that this group of creators from different countries ended up serving the interests of the bourgeoisie?

In general, and not only in the case of modernism, historians have limited themselves to analyzing artifacts of "high culture" as illustrations of sociopolitical development or as reflections of dominant ideology. But to analyze only the bourgeois aspects of literature is to impose a misleading homogeneity upon social discourse and assume that social classes have "pure," "necessary," or "paradigmatic" ideologies (Laclau, 105). Fredric Jameson in turn emphasizes that "the movement of the historical coexistence of various modes of production is not synchronous in this sense, but rather it is open to history *in a dialectical way*."[39]

The modernists entered the market as producers of ideology. "Ideologizing function" is the exact expression Rama uses to describe their social role in *The Lettered City* (110), but such an expression can lead to confusion, especially if we take into account that a large portion of the modernists' work was published not in the limited collections of their poetry but in the forceful daily press, with all the power that journalism has to shape the social imaginary.

The confusion regarding producers and transmitters of ideology stems from the idea, effectively refuted by Ernesto Laclau, that all ideology is dominant. We can also say that all texts are a symbolic act representing a broad, class-based collectivity, that the text is something more than an individual *parole*. Athusser has reworked the traditional marxist notion that there is no socialization that does not reproduce the modes of production, which would suggest that the modernists' texts were fated to reproduce the values of the market system (Althusser, 9). Althusser's theory does not take into account the fact that there are sectors of the population inspired by an ideology divergent from the dominant one, and that in every social system there are individuals whose task it is to oppose that system. Thus, in order to understand the ambivalent and heterogeneous "ideologizing function" of the modernists it is best to refer to a definition of ideology such as that proposed by psychologist Jacques Lacan: "Ideology is the means by which the subject attempts to breach the gap between private experience and the collective."[40]

All texts can be read as the writing of a pre-existent ideological or historical subtext, and as *a dialogue of social antagonisms*.[41] Jameson uses a definition—extremely enlightening for modernism—that designates a "cultural revolution" as the moment in which previously coexisting modes of production become clearly opposed or antagonistic. The vision of antagonisms can be identified with the *fin de siècle* Spanish American society and with modernist sensibilities: modernism can be seen as a significant ambivalent moment of resistance to the bourgeoisie.

This is not what Juan José Hernández Arregui thought. To him, modernist texts were "the luxury that the oligarchy adds to its upstart curiosity for culture."[42] José Luis Romero accuses them of being poetically idealized "crass parvenus" (290).

These ideas seem to coincide with our previous discussion of the modernists' relation to the bourgeoisie and their representation of the *intérieur*; they would seem to explain the apparent frivolity of many chronicles produced in Spanish America by the modernists. However, frivolity and luxury were also the "amusing envelope"—to use Baudelaire's expression—of a marginalized sector's spite. It was not for nothing that Gutiérrez Girardot referred to the modernists as "economic outcasts." This group, *pour épater le bourgeois*, appropriated elements of bourgeois culture precisely to express opinions against the bourgeoisie.[43]

Traditional Marxists consider writers as direct producers in the ideological sphere, creators of ideological-cultural goods.[44] But this definition is rigid, as Jameson has shown, because the idea of this type of goods contains the assumption of a univocal interpretation. As Foucault ironically commented, referring to those who lean on Marx, Hegel, and Freud, "their foolishness is to believe that all thought 'expresses' the ideology of one class" (328). Furthermore, as was discussed in the previous chapter, there was no hegemonic discourse in *fin de siècle* Spanish America, but rather several diverse discourses within the dominant class.

In the case of the modernists, it is clear that they adopted a semi-official posture of insulting the process of monetarization and reification.[45] Nonetheless, this is a very ambivalent issue: the literary revolution they produced profoundly changed Spanish American culture, which makes untenable the idea that they sided with convention. At the same time, it is undeniable that they sang the praises of opulence, repeatedly using adjectives like "select," "rare," "exquisite," "refined," and especially, "aristocratic." Today it is well known that their aristocratic inclinations were a way of attacking the vulgarity of the bourgeoisie. At the turn of the century, however, the bourgeoisie was not yet fully recognized as a distinct social group. They were frequently confused with the merchant class or the ruling elite, and as a result much of the modernists' critique was misunderstood. In any event, the aristocratic tone of much modernist writing tended to look down upon the popular classes as well, making the writers seem decidedly elitist.

Another aspect to consider is the presence of the suprareal in modernist literature, used as a way of overturning the dominant vision of the world. But it is also a way of evading reality, an interpretation supported by the fact that the majority of modernists stepped over and beyond the impoverished masses.

Real de Azúa also observed that, with their passion for brilliance, modernists exalted figures of real or potential heroes—and these were not always the best political leaders. But this tendency was based on their need for new men and went against the old oligarchy that supported the governments of their countries.

In their ambivalence they both warned against the dangers of imperialism and exalted the United States as a model of progress. In the spirit of universalism and search for the autocthonous, they—Martí included—found themselves idealizing Spain, "and it is difficult to know to what extent . . . they were conscious that with this position they validated the worst traditions of brutality, fanaticism, greed, hatred, and stupid arrogance, which they saw as 'noble,' 'romantic,' 'poetic,' and 'ideal'" (Real de Azúa, xxiii).[46]

Another of the accusations against modernism is that its proclivity for ornamentation was a mere exhibition orchestrated with the demands of the market in mind. Worse still is the suggestion that these writers, finding themselves overwhelmed by the laws of supply and demand that were imposed on many by the regular labor of journalism, were incapable of seeing that this labor provided them with new literary forms and instruments, such as the chronicle.

We cannot engage in anachronisms and expect the writers of the past to conceptualize genres the way we do today. Neither can we ask modernists not to view journalism as a form of slavery, or—like Gide—to understand that limits made them stronger.

What is most puzzling about modernists' objections to journalism is to define a situation they would have preferred:

Perhaps it was the situation of the financially independent man of letters in the Middle Ages or the Renaissance that Silva rather brazenly sought. Perhaps it was the status of the "Gray Eminence"; or perhaps the glamor of Goethe at the side of a benevolent dictator in some tropical Weimar. It could have been the patronage of some generous Mecenas, offered with no strings attached. At least Darío once imagined his destiny as such. (Real de Azúa, xvi).

There is prejudice in these comments. Despite the explicitly capitalistic discourse of some examples of modernism, we have no reason to believe that writers accepted the rules of the market so absolutely. After all, they could have insisted on a true professionalization in which they were adequately remunerated for their activities instead of aspiring only to the specialization of writers' work.

In order to reach some kind of conclusion, it can be said that modernist writers formed a poetic discourse that was less dependent on direct political praxis than other literary currents of the time. They sought to define literary discourse and to achieve professional status as writers by defending the rights of authorship.[47] It should also be said that in the late nineteenth century the figure of the writer did not have the same sophistication that his European counterparts acquired thanks to the highly public controversy surrounding the Dreyfus affair and the journalism of writers like Dostoyevsky, Marx, and Nietzsche. The Spanish American modernist's function with respect to the State was also not comparable to that of figures such as Domingo F. Sarmiento or Andrés Bello. Nor was the modernist contribution limited to the realm of literature; on the contrary, their work was central to Spanish America's cultural redefinition.

It is not a mere detail that the modernists linked social change to the goal of linguistically and syntactically renewing the Spanish language. José Martí made his anti-academicism explicit in his poetics. Rubén Darío stated that the "verbal cliché" locks in mental cliché, and together they perpetuate stagnation and immobility.[48]

The rupture of perceptive stereotypes and an increased flexibility in the interaction of messages that the modernists' journalism brought about makes it impossible to interpret modernism as a univocal movement. The reconsideration of modernists as writers who reacted critically to their society and its values is due in part to their work of renovating the language of the daily papers. The requirements of this medium brought them down from the ivory tower, forcing them to apply their new, autonomous literary discourse to the recording and interpretation of current events. For this reason, studying the chronicles reveals the biases inherent in calling modernism an evasive or elitist discourse without examining its contradictions. Since modernists viewed Spanish America as the recipient of universal culture, they have often been accused of importing and imitating foreign arts; on the other hand, their work laid the foundations of a practice that Fernando Ortiz and Angel Rama later designated *transculturation*. In other words, modernists established one of the most important strategies of Spanish American literature: their eclectic appropriation of elements from different cultures, traditions, and genres subverted the established literary order and ultimately created a new one.[49]

Chapter 3

The Emergence of the Chronicle

What then, you live on writing?
May God never allow it. I'd rather be a thief, it would be less despicable . . .
Here it is dishonorable to work with one's head, that is, like a man:
while it is honorable to work with one's arms and legs,
that is, like a beast.
—Juan Bautista Alberdi, alias Figarillo
(*El Nacional*, November 1938)

1. The Limits of Spanish American Journalism

From the post-independence period through the 1880s, Spanish American newspapers were a rationalizing force in the *res publica*. Commercial advertisements occupied little space, covering only curiosities and leaving competition up to oral advertising. This trend coincides with Sombart's description of Europe during the same period: "The distinguished publishers were averse even to the simplest commercial advertisements; publicity was held to be indecent."[1] Journalistic discourse during this period was directly linked to the public emergence of a group of "private persons," landed gentry and emerging cultured bourgeoisie, who came forward with economic agendas and plans for development. They legitimized their agendas using the language of reason and freedom of speech, which in their case meant nonintervention by the State. Their method continued through the modernist period.

For its first five years Argentina's *La Nación*, for example, founded in 1870, was a mouthpiece for the Partido Liberal. This party was dominated by the Mitre family, who were the owners of the newspaper. Bourgeois and political publicity did not, therefore, take separate ways. Journalism bore the stamp of the "party of notables," a group of educated and influential men that included clergymen, professors, lawyers, doctors, teachers, pharmacists, manufacturers, and landowners. They formed political clubs, topical coalitions, and electoral associations. The number of professional politicians was reduced during this period: for the "gentlemen," politics was a secondary occupation, but nonetheless officials rendered frequent reports to the newspapers.

Thus the project of "reason" was not limited to organizing information. Opinion played a fundamental part in these cultured papers, which were written, in large part, by writers. Such is the case with Juan María Gutiérrez, founder of *La Nación Argentina*, which directly preceded *La Nación*. A pedagogical spirit suffused these publications, which found public education and the consolidation of a national identity among their *raisons d'être*.

Newspapers are for modern people what the forum was to the Romans. The press has replaced the pulpit and podium, writing has replaced the spoken word, and the speech of the Athenian orator, delivered with the magic of gesticulation in order to move the passions of several million listeners, is pronounced today before millions who see it in writing, since distance keeps them from hearing it. Thanks to *journalism*, genius has the world for a nation and all of *civilized humanity* for witnesses.[2]

As Habermas has explained, with the consolidation of the bourgeois State, the press began to detach itself from the government and official opinions and began to attend to profits like any other commercial undertaking.[3] But in the case of Spanish America it is difficult to affirm that the birth of a commercial press is directly related to the "consolidation of the bourgeois State," since such a consolidation is questionable even today. Moreover, economic liberalism led to authoritarian regimes in many of the countries of this hemisphere, making it difficult to detach commercial enterprises from the State. What is true, however, is that around the decade of the eighties, the Spanish American press underwent a change similar to that of writers: both ceased to spread State discourse and began to propagate more independent ideas.

The history of *La Nación* shows a clear moment of change after the failed coup d'état against president Nicolás Avellaneda. The editorial line was forced to change in order to survive, since the owners entered into real conflict with political and State interests. Thus, in 1883, during José Martí's time as a correspondent in New York, the following *profesión de fé* (pronouncement of faith) appeared:

Since [the termination and imprisonment of Mitre], *La Nación* has outstripped the other newspapers in Bueons Aires. The administration gave the business [which had been exclusively political until this date] a commercial character. Without lowering its flag, the newspaper entered upon more solid ground, channeling itself into the analytical current from which it was estranged, and which is the main source that feeds journalism.[4]

By "commercial character" is meant more than simply the operation of a business whose product is news. By 1877 *La Nación* was Spanish America's most modern newspaper, having incorporated the telegraph and dedicated almost fifty percent of its space to advertising both national products for export and imported novelties from Europe and the United States. Thus, to speak of the commercial character of journalism at that time was to point to its commitment to commerce, not only through the profitable dedication of space to advertising, but also by referring to importing/exporting activities. Even Martí had to write advertisements for the daily *Las Américas* between 1883 and 1884 (VIII, 265–76).

Technology spurred further changes in journalism. Until this time, news had taken weeks to travel by boat: it was sent from France or England to Portugal, where it began its maritime route toward Buenos Aires, stopping in Rio de Janeiro and Montevideo. The instantaneity brought by telegraph was an incentive for internationalism and modernization, which dovetailed with the interests of the importing bourgeoisie. Internationalism was almost inevitable for the readers of *La Nación*. Since 1881, the newspaper had had correspondents in Africa (John Roe), in Peru and Chile (Brocha Gorda), in France (Ernesto García Ladevese), in Italy (Aníbal Latino), and in England (G. Z.). Argentinean current events were covered by Paul Groussac, a writer of French descent. *La Nación* tended to cover border information from Chile and Uruguay. But the rest of Spanish America, except for an occasional fact about the Panama Canal, was a largely missing element.

Newspapers changed slowly. The figure of the reporter emerged, as a direct result of the language of telegraphic notes. Manuel Gutiérrez Nájera complained: "The telegram has no literature, or grammar, or spelling. It is brutal."[5] Nevertheless, newspapers kept the editorial on the front page and continued to publish literary texts and pamphlets, especially translations. The "objectivity" of telegraphic notices shared space with scientific stories that seemed plucked from fantastical literature. One example of this kind of text, the tone of which is somewhere between ingenuous and jocose, is "A case of double life (a paper presented to the Psycho-cosmos circle by Dr. Camilo Clausolles) concerning an original case of fluid union between the existences of two twins which occurred in this city." It was published in two parts on April 10 and 12, 1881, and is not far removed from the imagination of Leopoldo Lugones's *Las fuerzas extrañas*. A similar resonance exists between Horacio Quiroga's short story "El almohadón de plumas" and the article "Una caso raro" (A strange case), which appeared in *La Prensa* (November 7, 1880). The boundaries between science and fantasy were blurry at that time.[6]

It is worth pausing to describe the front page of *La Nación* beween 1880 and 1895. One of the most notable elements is the layout: the bottom of the first page always offered a serialized novel, usually translated from English, French, or German. Occasionally a Spanish author was featured, but almost never an Argentine or Spanish American, unlike the first phase of this paper, in which preference was given to *costumbrista* authors, whose subject was the local culture.[7]

The layout of the serialized novel was distinct from the rest of the page. This was not true of other sections, since editorials, news, essays, and stories all shared the same format. The editorial was identifiable only because it was always placed in the first column; other than that, it was difficult to distinguish between fiction, opinions, and news stories, although the latter were often preceded by a summary. Fiction and opinion articles looked exactly alike, and a reader's possible confusion was made even likelier by the fact that news and literary stories were not always signed, or were signed merely with the author's initials.[8]

The brief and dry newsy style of some of the telegraphed sections was juxtaposed with long personal polemics belonging to another era in journalism—that of private persons rather than professional journalists. In October 1885 such a polemic took place for several issues between Domingo F. Sarmiento and Claudio Caballero over a personal quarrel, in the form of a private correspondence.

Spanish American journalism had not yet found its discursive autonomy. *La Nación*'s regular correspondents were essentially the great writers of the hemisphere. The very top writers, even in the simple terms of the amount of space they were given, were José Martí and Emilio Castelar. The illustrations—no photographs were published yet—did not help to distinguish between texts because they were limited to advertisements. The same was true in *La Opinión Nacional de Caracas*, where José Martí began his work as a correspondent and published some of his best chronicles.

La Nación also brings to light another instance of blurred discursive or generic boundaries: equal space was given to scientific texts, which today can be read as fiction, and political articles, which were read as pure literature at the time. Thus, when Martí described the presidential elections in the United States (1888), the editors of the newspaper titled his chronicle "Narraciones fantásticas" (Fantastic narrations) and added the following comment: "Martí has given us proof of the creative power of his privileged imagination here, sending us a fantasy that grabs the reader with its ingenious subject and an animated and picturesque scenic development. Only José Martí, that original and always fresh writer, would think to describe a society so ensconced in these ridiculous electoral functions in our advanced times" (XIII, 337). A study of the Caracas daily *La Opinión Nacional* between 1880 and 1883—when Martí maintained a relationship with that publication, be it as a reader, contributor, or correspondent—reveals similar generic confusions.[9]

Even with fewer of its own journalists stationed abroad, *La Opinión Nacional* emanated a sense of internationalism by reproducing articles from the *Times*, the *Hour*, *Paris Herald*, and the *Star Herald*. Literary translations and articles about important figures were centered on French, German, English, and Spanish cultures. The most cited and translated author was Victor Hugo, followed by Goethe. *La Opinión* shared with *La Nación* an interest in science, education, and the spirit "of freedom and progress of the United States." *La Nación*, however, often commented favorably on immigration in its editorials, whereas *La Opinión Nacional* had an ample section entitled "Anales Patrios"[10] (National annals), which gave more attention to local life and values. This was accomplished through articles about customs and manners—love and the family, for example—grammar, national literature, and Venezuelan history and the deeds of its heroes.

Other details include a smattering of similarities and differences. The advertisements in *La Opinión Nacional* were largely for health products, unlike those of *La Nación*.[11] The former was distributed regularly in Paris, London, and New York. It also included official documents and personal letters on the front page, such as the epistolary exchange between Vicente Coronado and Fausto Teodoro de Aldrey on the death of Aldrey's daughter on January 28, 1881. Among the contradictions of this publication, one of the most obvious is the frequent praise for Guzmán Blanco, the dictator who forced Martí out of the country in 1881. He was called "the illustrious," "the civilizer," "the creator of the glorious septennial," and ultimately even the hero of "forty years of combat between radical democratic ideas and conservative oligarchic principles, both pernicious extremes" (January 24, 1881). Blanco himself sent letters explaining his cause to *La Opinión,* with the understanding that they would be published.

Thus, state, private, and commercial expression all coexisted in *La Opinión Nacional.* An even more notable aspect of this mixing of genres and discourses was the blurring of boundaries between fiction and reality in which Martí was involved. One such example occurs in Martí's "Sección constante" (Constant section) in *La Opinión Nacional.* It almost seems like a fantastical story: "Thanks to the microphone, an English chemist has been able to prove that those miserable flies, for which we have no compassion and which so often perish at the hands of naughty boys, suffer as vividly as the most sensitive mortals. They express their pain in prolonged and anxious moans which the microphone distinctly transmits to the ear, and which sound like the neighing of a horse" (XXIII, 207).

The same period produced texts like "El rostro rehecho" (The remade face), in which literary style and descriptive charm far exceed the interest of the information. Here Martí describes the plastic surgery of a German servant girl in an almost playful recitation of this novel procedure:

They made an incision in the index finger of her right hand, that went from the first joint to the thumb; they put the right hand on the left arm, and after sewing the piece of skin on the incision in the finger with silver wire, they attached the arm and the hand with strong bandages. After a week, the piece of skin had grown on to the hand, although it was fed mostly by the arm. To change the flow of nutrition, they gradually cut the skin from the arm, and when it was about to separate, the skin was receiving its nutrients from the finger and not from the arm from which it had been taken. This separated it definitively from the arm. The hand, with the piece of hanging skin it was supporting, was taken to the patient's face. They lifted the scarred skin that covered her right cheek and injected the skin under it. With new bandages, they left the hand attached to the cheek . . . Today she walks around, lovely. (XXIII, 30–31)

This text, which begins with an ode to beauty as an expression of virtue, overcomes its unappealing subject matter and lack of newsworthiness compared to the events of international politics. Its value is strictly narrative.

These observations are crucial to our consideration of the chronicle as an intermediary between literary and journalistic discourses, but especially as a literary genre. We should recall some modernist texts that, after being published in newspapers, were stripped of their topical element and read as stories. This is the case with Gutiérrez Nájera's *Cuentos frágiles* and *Cuentos de color humo*, or Rubén Darío's "Esta era una reina," "¡A poblá!," "Bouquet," and "El año que viene siempre es azul"; or texts such as "El terremoto de Charleston" or "Jesse James" by José Martí.[12] Darío did not hesitate to publish his chronicles in book form; *Los raros* is surely the one that stands out the most.

Martí imparted precise instructions in his "literary testament" to compile all of his journalistic texts, which suggest how greatly he valued them:

Of the printed material, should it be necessary, material for the six main volumes could be chosen from the collection of *La Opinión Nacional, La Nación, El partido Liberal, La América, El Economista* . . . I have much work that is lost in countless papers: in Mexican papers from '75 to '77, in *La Revista Venezolana* . . . in papers in Honduras, Uruguay, and Chile, and who knows how many prologues. If I don't return and you insist on putting my papers together, make the volumes the way we planned. (I, 3–4)

2. The Professionalization of the Writer and Journalist

The contest between journalism and literature had begun. *La Nación* (1889) printed statements such as the following: "Journalism and letters seem to go as well together as the devil and holy water. The essential qualities of literature are, in effect, vigorous conciseness (invaluable in a long composition) and elegance of form . . . A good journalist, on the other hand, cannot afford to let his pen stray in fields of fantasy."[13] Until the eighties, newspapers were also the place for literary activity. Then the practice of writing became diversified, in order to compete in a new division of labor (Ramos, 159–60). Nonetheless, literary writers occupied a prominent place in the modernization of newspapers; *La Nación*, for example, introduced such figures as Martí, Darío, and Castelar in its pages. These additions were the source of prestige and more than a few conflicts because there was at the time a strong tendency not to sign articles with the writer's real name. Martí wrote for a time as "M. de Z." for *La Opinión Nacional* in Caracas; modernists tended to adopt such picturesque pseudonyms.

For example, Martí's first text for *La Opinión Nacional*, dated August 20, 1881, was published the following September 5. Within the year the editor of the newspaper, Fausto Teodoro Aldrey, sent Martí a letter. Once Aldrey had asked Martí to expand his works with international diversity and an ultramontane tone, but now his message was specific and direct:

[T]he public is complaining about your latest reviews of Darwin, Emerson, etc., because readers in this country want political news and anecdotes and the least literature possible. In this regard I am relegating [to a secondary position in the newspaper] the *Sección Constante* because people are grumbling about it, saying that it talks a lot about books and poets. Furthermore, the paragraphs are too long. This Section, which I would like to continue, must have short paragraphs.[14]

When Aldrey revealed to the public the identity of the successful and mysterious contributor "M. de Z.," he declared that Martí's style had "the clean cut and the brilliance of a diamond's radiance," but in another letter he reiterated the public's preference for subjects "more newsy and less literary . . . What is it they want? They do not make it explicit. I presume to guess." In that letter Aldrey asked Martí to make changes in his political judgments of the United States, a request that must have been familiar to Darío and Castelar as well.

Bartolomé Mitre had even less patience with political judgments that might displease the readers of *La Nación*. He did not hesitate to eliminate whole paragraphs of the texts Martí sent him from New York. But he at least admitted sincerely that the newspaper had become more commercial: "I hope you will not take this letter as the pretentious lecture that one writer delivers to another. Speaking to you is a youth who probably has a lot more to learn from you than you from him. But, dealing as we are with merchandise—and please forgive the brutality of the word, for the sake of exactitude—that needs to be placed favorably in the market which is the basis for its operations."[15] These letters reveal much: a formal, respectful, and almost admiring tone was maintained toward those who possessed literary talents. The words "market" and "merchandise" seemed brutal but were used anyway. Censorship existed as a means of commercial self-defense, a means not to distance the consuming public; it had nothing to do with avoiding reprimands from the State. The readers' interest in literature was as slight as their hunger for international news was huge. Brevity in writing was encouraged.

Perhaps most intriguing is the public/reader element, a determining factor in editorial decisions. Although editors did not pretend to understand their public very deeply, they did hope to interpret its tastes and desires. What's more, the pedagogical ideal of the press disappeared so thoroughly that Aldrey, in this same letter, says, "I don't know if I have correctly guessed the craving of this reading public, whose taste in this matter is perverted." The point was no longer to educate the perverted taste, but to satisfy it.

What did "satisfy" mean? According to Antonio Castro Leal, "the chronicle imposed the fundamental conditions of being easy to read and of attracting and interesting the reader. To be easy to read, it had to be written in a fluid, agile prose with no difficulty for the reader. In order to attract his interest it had to deal with current themes, offering, without fanfare, new points of view and original reflections that were discreetly suggested to the reader."[16] Martí himself, in a letter to Manuel Mercado, explains that he imagines himself seated at his table in New York, writing about political cases, social studies, reviews on letters and theater, and novelties, in other words, "all the things that could interest our educated readers, whether impatient or imaginative, but in such a way that it could be published in daily newspapers." Who were these readers? Obviously an elite of "private persons," but one that is larger than we might today imagine.

At that time, after Sarmiento's presidency, Argentina was famous for its obligatory literacy. But even in that country the numbers are misleading: though there were thousands of official students, the average school attrition was 90 to 97 percent during the last twenty years of the nineteenth century. A large part of that desertion occurred in the first or second year of instruction (Prieto, 28). The lack of education was not limited to Spanish America: school attendance in France and England averaged one to two years per child.[17]

Despite these numbers, the growth of Argentine journalism is impressive. In 1877 the number of dailies in circulation was 148, for 2,347,000 inhabitants; that is, one for every 15,700 people. The United States barely doubled these figures. Argentina took fourth place in the world in the average number of dailies per person, moving to third place in 1882 when the print run reached 322,500 copies per day, one for every nine or ten people. From 1887 to 1890 *La Nación* sold 35,000 copies a day.[18]

These figures, which reveal the vast size of the Argentine middle class, must have been attractive to modernists, whose "real and pathetic situation," as Rama has written, was the lack of an audience. As writers, they had few alternatives for survival:

The only modern and effective path was to sell the ability to write within a new job market that opened up at the time, *the writing market.* They found two principal buyers for their trade. One was politicians, for whom writers became scribes for their speeches, proclamations, and even laws (a task they continue to perform today). The other was newspaper editors, who, like politicians, frequently erased the writers' personalities by eliminating their by-lines. (*La ciudad letrada*, 122–23)

The literary quality of modernist chronicles must not be dismissed merely because these articles were remunerated work and submitted to editorial politics. The modernists themselves, through their abundant complaints, contributed to an early lack of critical interest in these texts. "The first thing done to a journalist when he takes his position, is to strip him of the most indispensable quality for a writer: his own personality," wrote Julián del Casal.[19]

And Rubén Darío said, "The literato can write a report: *the reporter cannot have that which is simply called style* . . . In sum: 'the literato should be paid for quality and the journalist for quantity; the first for art and ideas, the latter for information.'"[20]

Gutiérrez Nájera wrote:

The chronicle is, ladies and demoiselles, in these times, an anachronism . . . It has perished at the hands of reporters . . . The poor chronicle, slow as horses, cannot compete with those lightning trains. And what is left for us, miserable chroniclers, contemporaries of diligence, thus freely named? We arrive at the banquet in time for dessert. Shall I serve you, miss, a *pousse-café*? Is there any champagne left?[21]

Gutiérrez Nájera thus describes his work as a chronicler as like a trapeze artist swinging and twisting with "the subtle flourish of genius, mischievous allusion," and "capricious paradox." And, cruel with himself, he parodies his own alleged francophilia by writing in French that his purpose is to "*Amuser les gens qui passent, leur plaire aujourd'hui et recommencer le lendemain, voilà, mesdames, ma devise!*" Ibid., 10–11).

Martí also joined the chorus of modernist laments:

The daily writer cannot strain for sublimity, nor for extravagance. The sublime is the essence of life: the mountain culminates in a peak: the sublime is like the peak of the mountain . . . Only those who are truly their own masters can achieve that state perpetually . . . [The rest] must make use of it if it comes, but must never force it. Inspiration is a lady, who flees from those who seek her. The daily writer, who may be occasionally sublime, must content himself with being pleasant. (XXI, 254)

The modernists endorsed this complaint, but none denied the effort they put into their texts. Furthermore, this daily activity was certainly reflected in their creative work as a whole. "I spent my days in Buenos Aires writing articles for *La Nación* and verses that were later my *Prosas profanas*," wrote Rubén Darío in his autobiography.[22] More important, he confesses that "it is in that newspaper that I learned in my own way how to *manage style* and that was the moment when two very different men were my prose masters: Paul Groussac and Santiago Estrada, besides José Martí" (Ibid.). This confession is noteworthy because it belongs to Rubén Darío, who differentiated between the true writer and the mere reporter precisely by their management of style: style was no less than the essence of the specificity of literary discourse. Darío, the great aesthete, reveals that he learned this from journalistic prose.

Despite their complaints, Julián del Casal and Gutiérrez Nájera accepted that journalism, as Darío said, "constitutes a stylistic gymnastics." And Martí, who often wrote in great haste, was not always able to reread those chronicles Sarmiento and Darío so admired. He spoke of "those miserable scraps of newspaper that you admire," scraps that he even called "childish" with notes saying, "Do not even read what I'm sending." Yet, he suffered if his texts were not published: "The truth is that it hurt me not to see them published."[23]

The chronicle is truly the laboratory of modernist "style"—as Darío would say. It is the space where their writing was born and transformed, where the diffusion of a sensibility and a way of understanding literature took place. This understanding has to do with beauty, with the conscious selection of language, with the use of sensory images and symbols, with the mixture of what is foreign and what is local, of styles, of genres, of arts. Complaints aside, the poetic change took place in the newspapers, and it was there that some modernists assembled the best of their work.[24]

As we have already noted, the first pronouncement of a new poetics occurred in the press. In the editorial of the second issue of the *Revista Venezolana*, José Martí wrote what seemed to him to be the primer of modernist aesthetics. First, he stated his clear belief that every occasion merits a specific language.[25] But the ability to vary form and style is not the sole point. The writer must also adapt to signs of the time:

Every era expresses itself through the language it uses as much as through the events that take place in it. *No one should meddle in an age they do not know well.* This is the color, the ambiance, the grace, and the richness of style. *An Egyptian sky cannot be painted with a London fog; and the youthful verdure of our valleys should not look like the pale green of Arcadia or the lugubrious hues of Erin.* Sentences have their luxuries as we have clothing: some wear wool and some wear silk, and some are angry because they have wool and the other silk. So when did finesse become a bad condition?

Here he adds one of his central reflections:

[T]he writer, like the painter, must paint. There is no reason why one should use various colors and the other should not. Atmosphere varies by zones; thus language should vary by subject. *If simplicity is the recommended condition, this does not mean*

that the garment cannot have an elegant decoration. The writer will be called *archaic* sometimes, on the rare occasions when he writes to the director of the *Revista Venezolana*. Other times he will be called a neologue. He will use what is old when it is good, and will create something new when need be. There is no reason to invalidate useful words or to shy away from the task of giving new words to new ideas.

In the first issue of *Revista Venezolana* Martí lays out his motivations. His ideas exemplify the early spirit of modernism, before it began to weaken under the influence of decadence:

We must push the powerful American wave with our youthful shoulders . . . We must suppress all thinking that diminishes the portentous dimensions of our miraculous past. We must discover with the zeal of geographers the origins of this poetry of our world. Its channels and springs are genuine, longer and deeper than any other body of poetry, refusing to hide in those pallid books that come to us from tired lands. We must pick up, with the piety of a child and for our own sustenance, that dust of glory that is a natural element of our soil here.[26]

But then, why all the complaints? Perhaps because, in the end, the modernists themselves did not understand the true attainments of their professionalization and had been contaminated by bourgeois principles, according to which merchandise and art, the useful and the sublime, money and creation, were opposite poles. In fact, writers such as Calixto Oyuela argued that the true artist should never be paid. The artist was supposed to approach literature with "il lungo studio e il grande amore," without constructing "commercial markets for the valuation of their 'intellectual products'" (quoted in Rivera, 104).

Françoise Perús maintains that the insistence on distinguishing so carefully between poetic prose and journalism had to do as much with the survival of lordly values as with the will to defend the social status of the writer and the autonomy of artistic activity.[27] Her explanation is ambiguous. Perhaps Walter Benjamin is clearer when he discusses the "loss of aura" in the sense that Karl Marx uses "aura." As Benjamin explained, the rise of bourgeois capitalism had demystified and desacralized all the activities that were previously honored and revered. It had transformed the doctor, the lawyer, the priest, and the poet into its salaried workers. For Marx, aura was the symbol of that which separated the sacred from the profane, making a radiant halo around the figure that withstood the pressures of his environment. But with the emergence of the bourgeoisie, the arts, sciences, and social theories became mere modes of production (Berman, 4 f). Writers were no longer assimilated into the gentry, with which they were identified if only for cultural reasons, but with the modern working class, with which they had nothing in common but the fact that they all received salaries.

Creators saw their livelihood come to depend on the monetary success of their work, which was a traumatic novelty. The modernists—ordained in the priesthood of romantic art—faced the fact that they had to sell themselves, piece by piece. Their texts were a product like any other commercial article and they were exposed to fluctuations in the market, as we saw in the letter from Mitre to Martí. Or as Martí himself replies in another letter: "What greater torment can you think of than to feel yourself capable of something grand and live tied to the puerile!"[28]

But, market demands aside, Martí doubtless continued to commit himself to his journalistic texts with as much pulchritude as he confessed in the *Revista Venezolana*. We have already seen that Darío declared Martí's journalistic prose to be masterful. Sarmiento admired the Cuban's writing so much that he asked Paul Groussac to translate into French a chronicle "of such a rough, heady, electrifying eloquence, that it blossoms on high above our heads." He wrote that "in Spanish there is nothing that resembles the braying of Martí, and after Victor Hugo, France offers nothing of this metallic resonance." But Sarmiento also demanded that Martí, as a correspondent in New York, be "our eyes, to contemplate human movement where it is faster, more intellectual, more free . . . to show us the way." He praised Martí's work as a "publicist," but reproached him for the qualities that actually make the chronicle a literary genre: "I would Martí gave us a little less Martí, less of the Latin, of the Spanish, of the South American, in favor of a little more of the Yankee" (Quesada, 107, 113).

Martí seemed conscious of the fact that journalism provided writers with what the book market could not provide: the democratization of writing. In other words, modernists reached a greater public through a medium to which the middle classes as well as the elite had access. In the prologue to Pérez Bonalde's poem, he describes himself witnessing a "decentralization of intelligence" and writes that what is beautiful is "the dominion of all."

The problem is that finally, as we have seen, art was still intimately related with the idea of a minority, of the "elect." Only with hindsight can we see what modernists themselves did not: that in their journalism they were creating their own version of popular literature. At the very least, it reached far more readers than their poetic texts. If modernists themselves undervalued their journalism, it is probably due to the rapidity of the changes they helped bring about in aesthetic tastes and literary styles: while changing the values of Spanish America's literary culture irrevocably, they were themselves still somewhat rooted in a more traditional understanding of the distinctions between art and commerce, literature and popular culture.

It is true that the function of journalism was also in dispute. Although Martí thought that the press had the "extremely high mission" of explaining, strengthening, and advising rather than "lightly or frivolously commenting on events that occur," his contemporaries were skeptical of such instructive commentary. Joaquín V. González, for example, said in 1888 that "the press is a monster that devours enormous quantities of ideas in a single day," ideas which are later melted down and processed by journalists "as if in a factory."[29] González Prada's opinion is similar: "Journalism . . . diffuses a literature of clichés . . . Many are the brains that do not function until the newspaper gives them a jolt: like some sort of electric lamp they only turn on when the current flows from the central office."[30]

But theoretical formulations, such as the famous one by Marshall McLuhan that "the medium is the message," are still far off in the future. Martí insisted on a different type of attitude and objective, viewing reporter and writer as co-existing in the same space just as different kinds of journalism do. To him, not only did newspapers not cater to the laziness of the masses, but the paper's duty was to "create theater" for "the poor and the lazy." It should, "extracting from books, facilitate reading to the poor in time, or will, or money." It should be "useful, healthy, elegant, opportune, and brave" and should bring something to all who "might need some knowledge" (XVIII, 513).

Both positions must have held some truth. But it is the role of the writer within journalism that interests us here.[31] Although Casal said that newspapers stripped him of his personality, there is more truth in Darío's statement that modernist texts were clearly distinct from journalistic articles in their "style." Editorial pressures and limitations cannot be denied, and neither can the speed that the papers required. Chronicles are indeed *literature under pressure*, but this does not make them anything less than literature. How, then, to account for the quality of texts that have not perished? One characteristic of journalism is its temporality, not only of the referent but also of the interest it sparks in the reader. What to make of the care with which they were elaborated? Martí said, "A newspaper's being literary does not depend on how full it is of literature, rather everything should be literarily written. Each article should reveal the gloved hand that writes it and the unmarred mouth that dictates it" (XVIII, 513). In the heterogeneous discursive medium that journalism was, literati resorted to stylization in order to distinguish themselves from mere reporters. The specific literary subject that produced the chronicle was apparent. Thus the emphasis on "style" only acquires its weight in relation to the "anti-aesthetic space in which it operates. Style, at the end of the century, was equivalent to the specific literary subject, while the anti-aesthetic place was the newspaper" (Ramos, 178).

The daily was a new genre in which communication and creation, information, economic or political pressures, and art all seemed at odds. But they found resolution in the chronicle. So much so that although, as journalistic material, chronicles had to contain a high degree of referentiality and topicality (news), as literary material they have managed to survive through history long after the facts they address have lost all significance as current events.

An ironic description by Manuel Bueno helps to clear up some differences between writers and journalists:

When a writer with ideas, a little cultured and blessed with a nice lexicon, appears in a newspaper office, it is usually said of him with disdainful reticence that he is a literato. Later, when that writer has acquired a certain mental stagnation that inhibits his view of the varied spectacle of the universe, when his thoughts automatically stumble upon ready-made topics and phrases, and he roughs up his style with schematic descriptions of pedestrian events that take place in our society, then we end up saying about him that "he is a journalist." (Acosta Montoro, 89)

González Prada thought similarly: journalism frequently resorts to common ground, to the cliché. This is somewhat the difference that, much later, Roland Barthes would find between *écrivain* and *écrivant*.[32] True literature must include an index of originality, of the opposite of the cliché, that is, a new way of saying something.

Of course what the creators thought of their own work is always interesting, but as Walter Benjamin said, "Rather than ask, 'What is the attitude of a work to the relations of production of its time?' I should like to ask, 'What is its position in them?'"[33] What defines products is their social status and not the artist's consciousness of his activity.[34] Therefore what matters are not the modernists' complaints but the reality of their chronicles' mode of expression, the position they occupied in their time. Martí describes this well: "And in America a new people is already in bloom. They ask for weight in prose and naturalness, and they want work and reality in politics and in literature. They have tired of everything inflated, and hollow and rudimentary politics, and that false vigor of letters that recalls the daring dogs of that crazy Cervantes. This literary generation in America is like a fantasy" (Lex, I, 823).[35]

This new mode of expression was not only a question of style. The chronicle introduced modernists to a new genre, certainly; but it also involved a new awareness of their medium and the development of new forms of perception. In the end it changed even the conception of potentially poetic topics: the concrete fact, the prosaic, the quotidien, the momentary—all this can be converted into poetry, once it has been refined and transmuted by the "soul" of the poet.

But in the universal factory there is not a single little thing that does not contain all the seeds of big things. The sky turns and moves with its storms, through days and nights, and man revolts and marches with his passions, his faith and bitterness. When his eyes can no longer see the stars in the sky he turns to those in his soul. This is where intimate, confidential, and personal poetry comes from, a necessary consequence of our times. (VII, 224)

"There are no minor facts," "every day is a poem" (X, 250), commented Martí enthusiastically after one of his readings of the *Herald*. He added: "In a good paper everything excites and sparkles." Journalists are "true priests," helping societies to forge themselves from day to day in "the sparkling mosaic of newspapers." Newspapers can overthrow "the human jungle" (García Marruz, 194–95).[36] Once again we must leave aside Martí's professional lamentations, especially from the period after he had access to North American newspapers: if in 1875 in Mexico he still thought that the press was a mere vehicle for news with a moral purpose, in New York Martí proclaimed that "the press is [Da] Vinci and [Michaelangelo]."

Fina García Marruz addresses the incorporation of daily life to Martí's chronicles. If not for the newspaper, she asks, "what traditional poetic form would have been able to encompass such an expanse of life in its minute and grand happenings?" Even more important, she claims, "what is miraculous is that these verbal creatures, made to live for an evening or a morning, are still alive as if they had just left [Martí's] lips, with an unfading freshness. The humble 'chronicle' became in his hands an extraordinary artistic vehicle."[37]

Martí was not the only writer who turned the chronicle into something more than an urgent piece of journalism, but his was certainly one of the greatest talents. Testimonies and close readings clearly reveal his influence on the rest of the modernists. Some modernists expressed disdain for their breadwinning work, but as Benjamin observed, authors' opinions on their own writing matter less than the place and real use of these works, because "the author who teaches writers nothing, teaches no one. What matters, therefore, is the exemplary character of production, which is able first to induce other producers to produce, and second to put an improved apparatus at their disposal."[38]

The fact that poets read chronicles is important because newspapers were an extraordinary medium of communication and the means of diffusing new literature. Their influence worked in two ways. First, the modernists used their chronicles to introduce Latin American audiences to the European and North American writers they admired. Second, the very texture and structure of their prose demonstrated the new poetics.

Why then—it is worth asking again—is there such a resistance to discovering the full scope of the chronicle? We return to the bourgeois idea of the opposition between art and money, to the romantic belief that the development of art requires total independence and liberty, or to the Marxist theory that control over modes of production is equivalent to control over each product. These theories coincide in representing modernist poetry as an ostentatious ceremonial, with a socioideological function that satisfies the grand bourgeoisie's exclusivity rather than the daily life of the majority.[39]

Of course, control over a mode of production such as a newspaper does influence its output, and total liberty at the moment of creation would be ideal for the artist. But just as it is undeniable that the modernists were subject to editorial pressure, it is also true that this pressure was so often reiterated because it was generally disregarded. From the time Martí began his work as a correspondent in New York, he received letters with suggestions from his editors, but this did not lead him to sacrifice his writing in order to keep his job. What's more, he preferred to give up his post at *La Opinión Nacional* rather than satisfy the demands of its editor, Fausto Teodoro Aldrey, who had already canceled some of his contributions for the "Sección constante." From the beginning of Martí's work for *La Nación*, Bartolomé Mitre asked him to moderate his judgments about the North American system. But Martí continued to express his criticism and Mitre continued to use him as a correspondent. There were certain limits to journalistic freedom, but none as rigid as corsets which constricted all movement of the imagination and the word.

Thus we can take into account the unique exigencies of this new genre—the necessity of objectivity and faithfulness to external reality, for example—without discounting its literary merits. John Dewey has studied this in relation to the condition of art: "the intelligent mechanic engaged in his job, interested in doing well and finding satisfaction in his handiwork, caring for his materials and tools with genuine affection, is artistically engaged."[40]

True literature, as we have noted, must show signs of originality: the opposite of cliché, a new way of saying something. The modernist chronicle, with its transcultural appropriations of impressionism, expressionism, symbolism, Parnassianism, Kraussism, and the recourses of other arts including journalism itself, satisfies all Kant's requirements of a work of art: it is original and exemplary. The writing of modernist chronicles cannot be considered, strictly speaking, an imitation of anything. This work is the creation of an *eidos*, "one 'original' among many copies, because it sets and causes the rules and the new norms."[41]

The problem was that the modernists comprised the beginning of what would be the professionalization of the writer. Balzac, much more pragmatically, had composed a literary code that allowed the right to a pension to any writer who had published more than forty pieces per year for ten consecutive years.[42] Only much later would Spanish American writers accept their situation as culture's workmen, even though there were countries as sympathetic to their condition as Argentina, which in the mid-nineteenth century had incorporated an article protecting authors' rights into its constitution. Martí was conscious of these issues, as his interest in defending intellectual property attests: he voiced repeated protests in his correspondence with Manuel Mercado because about twenty newspapers reproduced his texts without paying him (albeit covering them with praise).

José Martí and the modernists created a new prose in Spanish America but did not feel rewarded as writers. As the narrator of *Amistad Funesta* says:

"They are taught to handle written and spoken language, as the only way of life, in societies where the delicate arts that stem from cultivating language do not have enough admirers, let alone consumers, to reward the intellectual labor of our privileged minds with the fair price of our exquisite work" (XVIII, 198).

3. Precursors of the Chronicle

The French and English sketch of life and manners is the chronicle's closest antecedent. Its best exemplars in Spanish are Ricardo Palma, whose *Peruvian Traditions* we will soon address, and Spaniard Mariano José de Larra. Both of these were at once critical and creative philologists interested in representing the human "types" of their national traditions.[43] These sketches used local language and colors to create *tableaux vivants* that were generally set in the past, although some of Larra's notes referred to his contemporaries. Like most literature of that time, they performed a rationalizing function by organizing the national imaginary.[44]

Another, equally important, antecedent is the French *chronique* of the mid-nineteenth century, especially the *fait divers* in Paris's *Le Figaro*. The *chronique* was the place for varied novelties and curious facts that lacked relevance enough to appear in the "serious" sections of the newspaper.[45] The chronicle therefore developed out of journalism, literature, and philology. Thus it introduces itself into the market as a kind of archeology of the present which is dedicated to small facts and whose purpose is not to inform but to amuse. By definition, its founders in Spanish America are Manuel Gutiérrez Nájera (In *El Nacional* in Mexico, 1880) and José Martí (in *La Opinión Nacional*, 1881–1882, and *La Nación*, 1882–1895), both of whom took writing beyond mere entertainment and imbued the chronicle with a literary flavor.

Gutiérrez Nájera's work resonates with the light tone of the *chronique*, with a worldly air and abundant gallicisms. But the writerly inclination of these texts brings them closer to literature so that, as we have noted, chronicles quickly began to take the place of the short story.

Martí, on the other hand, managed never to seem frivolous—not even in *La Opinión Nacional*'s "Sección constante," a sort of verbal variety show that he maintained from November 1881 to June 1882. With his proclivity for oratory, he weighed each word with a preciseness that included as many archaisms as neologisms. Martí was elegant and varied: he jumped from advice about sleeping in a hat, to new types of porcelain for a good tea set, to wars, the details of international politics, education, architecture, fashion, and especially scientific advances and literary values. He never ceased to reflect upon ethics and the human condition and he wrote always with careful images, exhaustive information, narrative grace, and a spirit in which the smallest details tended to crescendo into a harmonic and transcendent whole. Nothing was small or uninteresting. Nothing was ignored by the gaze of that chronicler, who found in everything some meaning for culture and the cities' inhabitants.

Variety was doubtless a challenge. Gutiérrez Nájera, in fact, saw it as an absurd demand, one which required that the journalist "cut himself up in a thousand pieces and still remain whole." Thus:

Yesterday he was an economist, today he's a theologian, and tomorrow he will be a Hebrew scholar or a baker. He must know how to make good bread and what the laws of evolution are. There is no science that he is not required to know, nor art whose secrets should escape his understanding. The same pen which last night drew a chronicle of dance or theater the night before must serve today to sketch an article on railroads or banks, and all of this without time to open a book or consult a dictionary.[46]

Although Martí had written as a local contributor for newspapers in Mexico and Caracas, his real work began as a correspondent in New York for *La Opinión Nacional*. He thus inaugurated this type of activity for Spanish Americans. He was more respectful of the need to inform the reader then Gutiérrez Nájera, but this did not keep him from dedicating the same care to his chronicles as to any other literary text: "It is my own fault not to be able to do anything in bits and pieces. I want to load small molds with the essence of things, and *make newspaper articles as if they were books*. This is why I don't write in peace, or in my true way of writing, except when I feel that I write for people who must love me. Whenever I can, in small successive works, I shape the exterior version of the work that is already complete within me" (XI, 65).

Although he maintained the variety and novelty of the French *chronique* in most of the "Cartas" sent for over a decade from New York to the Americas, Martí broke with the tradition of *Le Figaro* in some of his best works by treating only a single subject. These are his pieces on the Brooklyn Bridge, the Charleston earthquake, Emerson, Longfellow, Walt Whitman, and Jesse James.[47]

4. The *Costumbrista* Sketch

Among the conventions that Martí attacked was certainly the *costumbrista* sketch. This genre, dedicated to describing local customs, tended to freeze popular reality with its supposedly regionalist mimesis. *Costumbrista* sketches, the Spanish American precursors to the chronicle, were still being published in Martí's time. "To write is to populate," wrote Carlos Monsiváis, paraphrasing Juan Bautista Alberdi's famous phrase, "To govern is to populate." Monsiváis's phrase is applicable to these sketches because they—like their mid-nineteenth-century predecessors—helped to forge nations by describing and promoting lifestyles, reinscribing customs as civic rituals, and affirming nationality by explicating it. This is the rationalization of public space with which we are familiar.

In the modernists' conception the world—really the city—appears to be fragmented, contradictory, dubious. Other writers of the time, on the contrary, remained closer to previous propositions, whose spirit is summed up in this challenge by Monsiváis: "You are standing before a portrait of your country. Whether or not you are a catalogued archetype, you are a reader who moves among archetypes and, therefore, you exist doubly: verify (reflective) the moral achievement of the conduct of others and amuse yourself (frivolous) with the excesses of picturesqueness, vulgarity, or pretension."[48]

Peruvian Ricardo Palma is the best-known author of this type of writing. For Palma, who began writing in the post-Independence period, texts are a way to fill the void in cultural discourse with humor. Thus he reinvents or recreates history through chronicles which are not truly fiction, journalism, or strict history. In newspapers, he proposes a kind of national literature that is skeptical and very definitely anticlerical, but not altogether anti-institutional. His pieces attract the reader with pleasant instruction, a mixture of annals and newspaper serials that hold themselves to be true in essence if not in fact. Palma was a member of the Academia de la Letra (Academy of Language): he believed vehemently in preserving Castilian Spanish, although he did incorporate some Americanisms when necessary. According to Palma, habit would establish preferred terms in the general vocabulary, and their shared use would in turn form a part of the national identity, a version of the *como somos*, or "what we are like."

In 1883, when Martí had already published the basic texts of his new poetics, Palma continued to produce his jovial texts full of sayings, proverbs, couplets, epigrams, and theatrical dialogues. He actively intervened as a "spontaneous author" or popular storyteller, taking a historical episode or explaining the origin of a sentence, always beginning with ambiance, moving on to a historical digression, and coming around to the most important part, the moral. Palma felt it was necessary to re-educate the people in their own history, and he did so. Although he often located Peru's national origins in the colonial era, he focused largely on representing the Other, the individual who is not from the dominant group in economic, military, or religious terms. In "El mejor amigo . . . un perro" (The best friend . . . a dog) (1883),[49] the Other is a picaresque foreigner who ends up committing suicide. The anecdote allows the chronicler to bring out of oblivion many archaisms and especially popular terms such as "mixtureras," "pedir sencilla," "agua rica," "la laya," and "papel manteca" (249). The same device is used in "Fray Juan sin miedo" (The fearless Friar John) (271–73), in which—under the pretext of recording the misfortunes of a picaresque friar—

the narrator offers opinions on the story, told complete with songs and nick-names. He gives little prominence to historical facts and much more attention to the origin of the tale, especially if it has to do with old people's memories.

In 1899 Palma still had a similar style and objectives, but his role as "popular storyteller" allowed him to detach the text from history and concentrate on the legend. Thus, in "Los siete pelos del diablo" (The seven hairs of the devil), Palma parodies military language, rescues archaisms, cites popular refrains and cigarette brands, all to end with the jest, "Such is the traditional story of the seven hairs which make up the devil's beard, a story read in a contemporary palimpsest of sneezes and tickles" (361).

To understand what the representation of the Other meant to nineteenth-century writers in Spanish America one can look to the example of Domingo F. Sarmiento, for whom writing was modernizing, or mediating between civilization and barbarism (Ramos, 3–57). In order to modernize, those two conflicting worlds had to be brought into harmony. On one hand, there was an attempt to rationalize society by imposing ideas "that were far from praising any of those instructive and humanly natural affections of the soul." On the other hand it was necessary to incorporate the savage Other into the nation by transcribing the spoken word of those who were not part of literate culture. But the transcriber has never been neutral, and the words of the Other appeared as if transformed by distance and difference: subordinated to the norms of Western culture. Once written, these words enter the game of social rationalization, recognizing the conditions of possibility and the anticipation of another order.[50]

The *tableau vivant* or sketch of customs and manners is one manifestation of the project of subduing the heterogeneity of discourse. In the new order that results, the Other is subordinated to the discourse of civilization, to the spaces disciplined by law. This occurs in Palma's texts, as well as those by Cuban *costumbrista* writers of the 1880s including José Quintín Suzarte, José E. Triay, Francisco Valerio, and Francisco de Paula Gelabert. In Quintín Suzarte's "Los goajiros," the description is drawn *d'aprés nature,* as if it were a picture with sound. The theme is the disappearance of traditional rural life in the face of "railroads, telegraphs, telephones, and all the other delights of civilization" (Bueno, 415).[51] All of these changes are part of the process of democratization and for that reason supposedly eliminate social classes. But as Quintín Suzarte suggests, they in reality only degrade the lower classes by stripping away their natural charm: the poor become merely *imitative* and lose their beauty. There is a strong sense of nostalgia for the past and a desire to preserve local words, colors, and customs.

In Quintín Suzarte's formulation, the natural man—the creole descended from European ancestors—is full of qualities that need to be civilized. This is not a matter of imitating appearances or of using hard work and education to turn the *goajiros* living in moral chaos into a distinguished family. José E. Triay's "El calasero" (The coachman) also uses many descriptive adjectives and regional terms, but it is even more deterministic than "Los goajiros." As in Quintín Suzarte's work the plot is practically non-existent, but historical facts are presented by a narrator who is both witness and authority, knowledgeable at once in popular customs and more cultured subjects. His language is functional, organized around an idealized upper class and a world that is being erased: the bucolic charm of the lower classes is being supplanted by the virtues of education and progress. Valerio's "¡Zacatecas!" stands out for its sense of humor. The narrator repeatedly appeals directly to the reader for comment on the text, addressing alternately his own social class, the Zacatecas, funeral directors, and citizens of foreign nations. "¡Zacatecas!" parodies the concept of modernization by translating "modernity" into a series of brand names, but there is an even greater rejection of certain customs that are seen as impediments from the past. This is combined with an albeit rather ironic belief in "the grandiose obelisk of progress" (433). De Paula Gelabert's "La mulata de rumbo" is born of the same rationalizing spirit, but is closer to naturalism in vision: the Other, "the inferior, uncultured being," is no longer a savage who must be civilized, but rather one whose misery is determined by his or her social environment.

Other variants are the Mexican chroniclers of the time. Guillermo Prieto's "La invasión yankee" (The yankee invasion, 1875) and "El grito" (The scream, 1849) also deal with representing the Other, but this time from within. In these chronicles the narrator is both character and witness. These are historical fictions created with realist description. They privilege narration but contain a sharp critical message in their condemnation of imperialism. They emphasize creole elements and represent the past in terms of the elite's interaction with the common people, representing national unity as a defense against the threat of foreign influence. Although Prieto's language is more narrative, the essential difference between his and other *costumbrista* sketches lies in the text's ideology rather than the narrative perspective and system of representation. This is not so in the case of Ignacio Manuel Altamirano's "Una visita a la Candelaria de los Patos" (A visit to the Ducks' Candelary, 1869). Altamirano's narrator shares a certain intimacy and even complicity with his readers by assuming their equality in culture and social class. The Other, however, is definitely society's outcast, forgotten by progress and in need of its assistance; the idea that progress or modernization must incorporate its outcasts is the theme of this chronicle. By just grazing the belt of misery that surrounds Mexico City without penetrating its squalid conditions in depth, the narrator denounces the current situation and suggests the clean-up of an area that is "the focus of the fevers that occasionally ravage the elegant parts of the city."[52] Another contemporary Mexican chronicler, Angel de Campo, employs a totally different system of writing. His "El fusilamiento" (The execution, 1894) describes a man's death with such impressionistic pleasure that the action seems suspended, in other words the effect is so strikingly visual that the text seems to lose narrative movement. For de Campo the topic is but a pretext: his objective is to describe meticulously rather than to tell or communicate. The military is represented, as well as the common people who witness the execution, and three representatives of the new urban institutions: a friar, a soldier, and a reporter, who appear in an automobile. There is a symbolic opposition between the train and the wife of the executed man, who "galloped desperately, carrying on her back a child who laughed tugging on her braids . . . The engine whistled once more from the curve, and its tuft of smoke, after floating slowly in the air, fell on the plain under the brilliant sunlight of a happy, blue spring day."[53]

5. Martí and the Press in Spanish America

As Monsiváis said, to write in Martí's time was also to populate and to civilize. But this nineteenth-century tradition was much more compatible with the projects of the bourgeoisie than most modernist work was. Although not all of the authors cited here shared the taste for importation that the bourgeoisie and the modernistas had in common, it should be said in general terms that their texts—the *costumbrista* sketches—were less critical of the dominant institutions of nineteenth century society. Believers in order and progress, they expressed the convincing logic that modernization should be offered to the Other as well. The eminent Eugenio María de Hostos, for whom literature had no function outside of educating and moralizing, maintained the civilization/barbarism dichotomy. His pedagogical "Retrato de Francisco V. Aguilera" (Portrait of Francisco V. Aguilera) practically speaks in the rhetoric of the Enlightenment. The discursive field is occupied by a defense of reason, law, the family, friendship among men, and the struggle for the fatherland. The subject of the portrait, Francisco V. Aguilera, represents the very best of the populace (Monsiváis, 126–27).

Although José Martí's interest in appropriating foreign elements may seem antithetical to literary regionalism, he nonetheless deeply recognized the need to produce a local literature in each country.[54] But, for him, authentic creation did not consist of drawing human types, exotic scenery, or legacies and decrees, as so many nineteenth-century Spanish American writers did; neither should the writer confirm or postulate philosophical, political, or religious systems of any kind, or trap reality in Eurocentric terms such as the opposition between the civilized and the barbaric.

Sometimes Martí drew human types according to their nationality in his chronicles: this is the case, for example, in "Un funeral chino" (XII, 77–78), in the masses portrayed on Brooklyn Bridge, or the series on the anarchist strikes by the "Caballeros del Trabajo" (Knights of Labor) in 1886, in which German immigrants are not treated kindly. But prejudices aside, the representation of national "types" was not the objective of these texts. In general these touches are given in passing, as another brushstroke in an impressionist painting. If Martí tried to delineate a human "type," it was one that could rise up as a modern-day hero. To this end he went beyond geographical limitations and tried to understand—from orators, writers, politicians, philosophers, and military men—the internal drive that moved them to search for the sublime in the midst of industrialization. These "types" did not exist solely through their dress or habits, as in the *costumbrista* texts, nor are they a metaphor for the people. They exist through their passion for what is great, for Liberty or Nature, for their ability to transcend mediocrity. Each "type" is elaborated from a real personality, but one whose specific biography does not matter much; what matters is creating an example. As Martí said, "I don't care about the stops along the human railroad that rise up and destroy the conveniences of the living. I care about the steam, which is changeable but free, that keeps the train moving" (XXI, 186). That is why the accumulation of concrete referential facts is not essential in his chronicles. Martí's system of representation differs not only from the system of the other chroniclers, but also from the other pieces published alongside his own. In reviewing *La Opinión Nacional* from 1880, for example, it becomes clear that this was still the newspaper of the illustrious, the medium for a certain ruling, liberal class to promote its ideas. It had not yet been "professionalized" as a newspaper, as it would later, in the sense of selling information.

Although it is true that the wirecopy in *La Opinión Nacional* consisted of news briefs, many of its texts were still editorials. On January 16, 1880, the paper reran a piece originally published in *El Hispanoamericano* entitled "Exterior—México, en la actualidad" (International news—Mexico today). The piece's style is characterized by short sentences, few adjectives, and a focus on facticity; its content covers many of the obsessive themes of Martí's work: the crisis of contemporary life, North American imperialism, the necessity of creating new and self-sacrificing men. The writer invokes the image of Christ, even to the point of calling Bolívar "the Christ of the Southern redemption" in order to suggest continental unity. America is represented as "Paradise awaiting a new Adam." This new Adam at first appears to be a figure for education, but in the end it represents instead progress, civilization, and commerce: all three embodied in the dictator Porfirio Díaz. This writer has in effect reversed Martí's strategy: rather than positing a contemporary figure or event as a pretext to speak of values and ideals, the writer of "México, en la actualidad" appropriates philosophical and political issues as a rhetorical base from which to launch his support of Díaz.

Other texts in *La Opinión Nacional* in Caracas, such as the reflections about the United States published on the front page on March 9 and 10, are similar. The main thrust is progress, education in terms of European and North American culture, reason, commerce, and industry, and the threat of imperialism from the northern neighbor. The language is functional, supported by authorities such as Hugo and Gautier, and has the same objective: to offer the populace the necessary education and work to accompany modernization.

The front page articles published until 1882—such as "Los partidos políticos (Political parties) (August 25, 1881), or "La libertad de prensa" (Freedom of the press) (February 25, 1881)—are unsigned and take an editorial tone, but are presented in the format of news. The outlook is consistent: civilization equals well-being, and we need to harmonize social relations, as if between associates in a mercantile company. Nature made man free; in order to maintain that freedom, the State must take care of it through laws, which are the arms of reason, and of the morality that channels the otherwise uncontrolled masses. A redemptional and positivist spirit infuses all of this.

The papers of the time presented a panorama of rationalizing discourse whose insistence on educating for progress seems like an imposition of foreign norms and a struggle against local reality. Martí responds to this positivist clamor by editing the *Revista Venezolana* in Caracas, a magazine dedicated to celebrating Venezuela itself, praising its heroes and its nature in a new language and defining the local not in terms of civilization, but rather as memories of the nation and its past. He posits tradition as art, book, man, landscape and color. He declares his isolation from the passion of domestic politics and his dedication to grander things, to the superlative, to the poetry of the new world, "whose genuine channels and sources, more natural and profound than those of any poetry known, certainly do not hide in those pale books, *feeble books that come to us from worn-out lands*" (my emphasis). He is also connected with the Bolivarist tribunal, but his hope is to find freedom and new divinities in Nature and in local history. At first glance it seems like a joke of extreme idealism, but his project is so radically opposed to the institutional power that the *Revista Venezolana* hardly makes it to its second issue: in the first, Martí had praised the writer Cecilio Acosta, who was considered an enemy by the dictator Guzmán Blanco. The note is enough to justify Martí's expulsion from Venezuela and inaugurate his long career as a correspondent.

La Opinión Nacional also employed a great correspondent who signed his work "Hortensio." His "Revista de política europea" is an assemblage of information and liberal opinions presented without narration, as in a news brief. Physically, his "Revista" resembles Martí's North American scenes—having the form of letters to the editor that are signed, dated, and preceded by a summary—but, unlike most of Martí's chronicles, which presented an outline made up of subtitles, Hortensio offered a true summary, albeit written in a telegraphic style. Here is one of Hortensio's summaries, from February 18, 1880:

SUMMARY

Spain.—Issues in Cuba.—Abolition Law.—Economic reforms on the island.—Return of the estranged members of Congress.—Financial situation of Spain and Cuba.—The regicide Otero is declared an imbecile by doctors.—Bolivia and Spain.—The Empress Eugenia.—Political situation in France.—Death of Jules Favre.

The following is by Martí, for the same newspaper, May 19, 1882:

EMERSON

Death of Emerson.—The great American philosopher has died.—The philosopher and poet, Emerson.—His pure life.—His mind, his tenderness, his fury.—His house in Concord.—Ecstasy.—The sum of his merits. His method.—His philosophy.—His extraordinary book: "Nature."—What is life? What is science?—What does Nature teach us?—Philosophy of the superhuman and of the human?—Virtue, the final objective of the Universe.—His way of writing.—His wonderful verses.

Martí's summary more closely resembles the kind of headings that preceded novel chapters in the nineteenth century, listing the sections that make up the whole, rather than summarizing the information. In fact, although it fulfills the basic requirement of giving the news of Emerson's death, this is later repeated, suggesting that the summary was not meant as a text with autonomous value, as Hortensio's was, or a regular journalistic summary. Rather Martí's is absolutely dependent on the text, a small index of its contents.

Comparing *La Opinión Nacional* with the Buenos Aires paper *La Nación* yields similar results. Despite *La Opinión*'s commitment to becoming commercialized as an informative medium, it long remained the place where celebrities voiced their opinions. Although *La Nación* concentrated on Argentina's national issues—the problems of immigration and populating the wild—its general thrust was the same. From the position of a privileged "we," *La Nación* called for progress, promoting social equilibrium as well-being and "fair play" and stressing the need to control chaos with the laws of conscience and reason. Once again the theme is to impart habits of order and freedom to the masses.

With this editorial position, *La Nación* published a mixture of news and editorials, international news briefs, chronicles, stories, serialized novels, and personal letters. One of these texts calls attention to itself for two reasons: first, the late date of its publication, and second, the identity of its author. The piece was published on October 18, 1885, by which time journalism had supposedly been modernized and, thus, depersonalized. The author is Domingo F. Sarmiento.

The author casts himself as the first-person protagonist who emerges in all of his colossal grandeur as he degrades his opponent, an ex-disciple whom he answers in this letter. His strategy is satire: he says the opposite of what he means at every turn, with the reader's complicity. He resorts to expressions in other languages and foreign turns of phrase (*speech* [in English], *homo, si jeunesse savait, flirteo, dollars, passe partout, gentleman*), citations of European authorities but especially of himself, colloquialisms, opinions, and statistics. He narrates, writes history, cites various letters he has received, and describes characters using their appearance to indicate their personality or condition. He insists on educating and civilizing and attacks the clergy and barbarity, all in an amalgam of styles that skips from correspondence to oratory, to the essay, and back to the letter or the anecdote.

Sarmiento never became a proper chronicler during Martí's time, although he occupied extensive space on the front page of *La Nación*. One who did share the chronicler's role with Martí, was the Spaniard Emilio Castelar, a foreign correspondent and literary writer as well. Castelar practiced the poetics of the new era, or so one concludes after a glance at a text such as "La leyenda de la ciencia" (The legend of science), published in *La Nación* on January 30, 1885. It abounds in images and comparisons, such as: "Poetry resembles will-o'-the-wisps in that it runs only through cemeteries and is crowned only with the willows and cypresses of death." He constructs natural analogies and attacks realist art and materialists in order to defend the connection between body and soul and a transcendence into the heavens. He works with oppositions and immediacy, and makes the muse-museum obvious. He touches on Christian and pagan mythology, exoticism, and illustrious North American men. He unites science and nature poetry, as in "when the stars descended into telescopes, like ships to their nests."

A bit of everything can be found in "La leyenda de la ciencia," except for a system of representation. It is a kaleidoscope that represents absolutely nothing. It is pure form without content, a combination of words in the new literary fashion. The more inflated the language, the more devoid of creativity it seems. Castelar uses more than thirty thousand words to express, basically, the unity of science and poetry. Marcelino Menéndez Pelayo satirized Emilio Castelar thus: "a great metaphor-hunter, inexhaustible in enumeration, a slave to the image who ends up choking the idea in the rings of his circumlocution, an orator who would have scandalized the supremely austere Demosthenes" (Menéndez Pelayo, 370).

To judge from the position given to these articles by Castelar, his rhetoric, unfortunately for literary history and for the chronicle, was judged equal to the brilliant innovations of Martí's prose. Many subsequent writers of this ilk, especially among Rubén Darío fans, would continue to confuse the reader and themselves with textual kaleidoscopes of luxurious wording and exotic images.

Such writing detracted from modernism's reputation for quite some time, but it did nothing to diminish the force of the movement's literary innovations.

6. The Chronicle as a Genre

Now we must consider why the chronicle is a literary genre in its own right, though it was first published in the press and satisfied the requirements of journalistic discourse. The criterion of truthfulness is an element that leads to confusion when classifying genres of writing. According to Aristotle, poets were liars par excellence and should ensure the verisimilitude of their inventions. Of course, the verisimilitude of a written word is a narrative element that should not be confused with truth. Since verisimilitude is in actuality only a literary or stylistic effect, one cannot come to the conclusion that fiction pertains to literature and truth to journalism.

When journalism began to define itself as an autonomous discourse, it established its domain in the realm of the *factual*, just as literary discourse established itself in the realm of the aesthetic. This distinction, of course, was a recourse of legitimization and differentiation. The writing strategy we know as "objectivity" did not take hold in journalism until the consolidation of international news agencies in the twentieth century.

Literary criticism has in general perpetuated bourgeois attitudes. By overlooking historical data such as those just mentioned, criticism at the end of the nineteenth and beginning of the twentieth centuries formulated a system of generic categorization that omitted the chronicle because it belonged to the factual realm. It was as if only the aesthetic and the literary could use imagery or allude to emotion.

Systems of representing reality are aimed at the public space, and their deployment has been determined since the turn of the century by the categories of truth/falsehood that are imposed upon journalism and literature. Creativity has been seen as the exclusive providence of a universe that lives and ends in and of itself, and it is still customary to evaluate the "literary" value of a text in inverse proportion to its connection to concrete reality. This line of reasoning has both hindered the recognition of the chronicle as literature and done injustice to good journalism.

The real referent has been confused with the system of representation, the idea of the fact with that of its narration. Raymond Williams argues, "The dichotomies fact/fiction and objective/subjective are then the theoretical and historical keys to the basic bourgeois theory of literature, which has controlled and specialized the actual multiplicity of writing" (Williams 147–49). Identifying the aesthetic with the fictitious has distanced literary discourse from the world of facts, making it seem a supplementary and unnecessary activity.[55]

Factuality should not, as a criterion, include or exclude the chronicle from literature or journalism. Real requirements for the chronicle are its referentiality—although it may be expressed by a literary subject—and its temporality: it must be current. Ortega y Gasset said that journalism is "the art of events as such." The chronicle, then, was a story about contemporary, everyday history.[56] What could be better for a literature such as the one to which Martí aspired than to "reflect in itself the multiple and confused conditions of the time, condensed, unprosaic, essential, and informed by great artistic genius" (XXI, 163)?

The text's autonomy within the aesthetic-literary sphere depends on neither the referentiality or topicality of the subject. We have noted that many modernist chronicles detached themselves from temporal elements and continue to be valuable as textual objects in and of themselves. In other words, having lost over the years the primary significance that the chronicles had for their readership of the time, they remain literary discourses par excellence.

Literary discourse is characterized by the preponderant role that is granted to contextual meanings.[57] The same occurs in regard to poetic language, so chronicles cannot be seen only as journalism, but must be considered poetic prose as well.

It is of less interest to define the expression "poetic prose," which suggests a false opposition between prose and poetry, than it is to rescue the notion that chronicles are also poetic discourse. They display the relationship between topical specificity or preciseness and intratextual resonance. A pair of examples will suffice:

He was born in a mysterious country: the earth's soul revealed itself to him in infancy, in its most enigmatic manifestations. Today he is old already; much snow has fallen on him, glory has hung a halo around him, like a magnificent aurora borealis. He lives far away, in his land of fjords and rain and mist, under a sky of fickle and evasive light . . . Great visionary of the snow! His eyes have contemplated the long nights and red sun that bloodies the winter darkness. Then he looks at the nighttime of life, the darkness of humanity. His soul will be embittered until death.

No, he is not of those who set a miserable thought loose, to stumble and drag along under the visible opulence of its splendid clothes. He does not inflate swallows to make them seem eagles. He showers down eagles every time he opens his hand, like a sower showers grain.

The first paragraph is from a portrait of Ibsen by Rubén Darío, from his series *Los raros* (199). The second is a homage to Walt Whitman by José Martí, from his letters from New York (XIII, 139). In both cases, if the graphic distribution were broken up and the prose distributed as verse, couldn't they be read as poems? It could perhaps be said that graphic distribution could transform any text thus, even the most banal. But what is true is that both paragraphs—or stanzas, to prolong the test—satisfy the conventions of lyric poetry in a narrative mode: they are atemporal, complete, coherent on a symbolic level, and express an attitude.[58]

The categorizing of chronicles is complex and fascinating. As the intersection of journalistic and literary discourses, they present two types of meaning: centrifugal and centripetal, or external and internal.[59] This represents the apparent contradiction that linguistic signs are at the service of the circulation of meaning within the text, while at the same time, they cease to be transparent, literal, or instrumental, and acquire specific and interdependent weight.

What is it that makes these informative, newsy texts "works of art"? What distinguishes and constitutes them stems from the will to create literature, surging especially from the way in which discourse is verbalized, how verbal art dominates the transmission of a referential message.[60]

Defining the chronicle genre as the coming-together of literary discourse and journalism is central to our investigation of Martí's work, as is understanding modernism's role in literary history and the renovation of Spanish American prose which the modernists actualized through print journalism. Genre is not a single aspect of a work of art, but rather "the whole utterance," because it determines both the form and the thematic result of the text, be it a detective story, scientific essay, or gossip column. It conditions what Bakhtin called the *chronotope*, the special relationship between space and time in any given text; the semantic axes (such as death or sex), the external orientation or conditions of perception and actualization, and the internal orientation of the text, the portions of reality of interest to that genre.[61]

Readers recognized the modernist chronicle as a genre in itself, distinct from pure journalism. There are abundant indications of this in literature of the time, including the previously cited example of Bartolomé Mitre: as editor of *La Nación*, Mitre felt justified in entitling a political note "Fantastic Narrations" simply because its author was known as a literary writer and therefore incapable of representing reality faithfully.

The chronicle is thus a genre and the intersection of two discourses. It is important to keep in mind that the genre is not politically neutral, and therefore the very choice of the chronicle as a writing tool takes the writer far from the ivory tower and the luxurious margins of society.[62]

Once again Martí finds an appropriate way to speak of the chronicler, although his words refer to Emerson: "He did not fake revelations. He did not construct mental worlds. He did not place mental will or effort in what prose and poetry he wrote. All his prose is poetry. And his poetry is prose—they are like echoes . . . He saw himself as a transparent pupil that saw it all, reflected it all, and was just a pupil" (XIII, 19).

Chapter 4

Writing the Present

1. Time as Poetics

José Martí's prologue to "Poema del Niágara" by Juan Antonio Pérez Bonalde (VII, 221–38) is a ground-breaking text because its aesthetic purpose is the representation of *temporality*, understood as the awareness of the present time.[1] Written in 1882, it attempts to define a local system of representation that expresses man's modernity in the Americas. It is a system capable of authentically apprehending the present. It is not an attempt to form a national essence through literature, but to acknowledge the crisis and hope of the *fin de siècle*. It aims to rediscover, through everyday language, the new relationship between man, nature, and the interior of each. Literature must be "our time, facing our Nature" (VII, 223).

Conventions of the past are hollow and foreign masks: "This century has worm-eaten walls, like a kettle in which metal has been liquefied," he says in "Las grandes huelgas en Estados Unidos" (The great strikes in the United States) (X, 411). A new man must be constructed, but Spanish America cannot be trusted to do it, even in its "quite confused budding institutions" (VII, 229). Everything must be relearned and rediscovered. This epoch, he assures us, is a period of the "dismembering of the human mind. Others were times of erected fences. This is the time of broken fences" (VII, 226). The chronicle "Coney Island" expresses the amazement Martí felt before the urban multitudes and constant social transition: "what amazes there is the size, the quantity, the sudden result of human activity . . . those roads that from two miles off are not roads but long carpets of heads. That mobility, that gift for advancing, that attack, that change of form . . . that crushing and uncontrollable expansiveness, firm and frenetic, and that naturalness about the fantastic . . . (IX, 125).

For Martí, this was a moment of constant development. The daily dynamic was such that man went to bed with one idea and awoke with another. Everything was fertile and fragmentary, vertiginous and imperfect. Speed, simultaneity, and the immediacy of what is human are the central issues. As Martí states, ignorance is shameful, and new answers are required: "Today no one has secure faith . . . [The interior of men conceals] Angst, Insecurity, Vague Hope, Secret Vision . . . What a fright to the heart! To ask for what is not coming! Not to know what we desire! To feel delight and nausea in our souls at once: nausea at the dying day, and delight in the dawn!" (VII, 225).

Fear and delight imply that doubt, transition, and amazement are all part of this perception of the world. Institutionalized traditions are not enough to understand life in its multiplicity. Science illuminates only partially the physical dimension. Metaphysics, especially ontology, is the branch of knowledge most bruised by modernity. One of the most transparent images is the representation of the lone individual among the multitudes of New York—the epitome of the new urban reality frightened by the monetarization of life and the loss of the meaning of existence.

New forms had to accompany the new processes of production. There were no longer truths like temples. Some partialities generated others. There was an urgency to understand a present to which a new piece was added every day. This is why José Martí concludes in his prologue to "Poema del Niágara" that the place for ideas is in journalism, the space of what is non-permanent, of communication, of new facts, of a public majority, a place to inquire and not to establish.

The newspaper is the sign of the new times. To a period of such mobility, corresponds a similarly mobile writing. Only journalism permits the invasive entry of life, and life is the only legitimate topic of the *fin de siècle* culture. Journalism was one of the natural formative sources for this new sensibility, which had to find poetry in an invasive dailyness. In the prologue to Pérez Bonalde, Martí explains the system of representation through the symbol and analogy, as well as the chronicler's work with vulgar and common material: "In the universal factory there is not a single little thing that does not contain all the seeds of big things" (VII, 224). He writes:

All is expansion, communication, florescence, contagion, and spread. The newspaper deflowers grand ideas. Ideas no longer form a family in the mind, or a household, or a *long life*. They are born astride a horse, on a lightning bolt, with wings. They do not evolve in a single mind, but by the consortium of all of them. Rather than taking long in benefiting a small number of readers after a belabored start, they benefit them instantly. Ideas are squeezed, held on high, worn as crowns, pilloried, erected as idols, overturned, tossed about. (VII, 227)

The modernist chronicle as a cultural practice reveals a deep epistemological fissure. Not only did doubt occupy the center of thought, but temporality invaded everything like a dizzy spell. Everything was fleeting, changing, and imperfect. It was the beginning of democratization and mass culture. "This is like a decentralization of intelligence. Beauty has become everyone's domain. Genius is moving from the individual to the collective" (VII, 228).

The forces of purist and pre-Raphaelite exquisiteness, Parnassian perfection, romantic meaning, positivism, and naturalist realism were all at work. In the midst of these, Martí proposed neither an escape to an interior still uncorrupted by material voracity, nor the reproduction of prestigious artistic canons. Instead he sought to incarnate himself in modernity, using and combining whatever he could to find the most sincere expressive form to give an account of the soot and vertigo of big cities. In his texts, and especially in his chronicles and poems, he rejects the customs imposed by urbanization and the bourgeoisie. As a poet-journalist, however, he denies that poetry might have collapsed along with traditional beliefs. Poetry—he exclaims—"is in the meltings and in steam-engine factories; it is the reddish and Dantesque nights of the modern Babylonic factories; it is in workshops" (XIII, 421).

2. Martí's Chronicles *vis à vis* the North American Press

Around 1890, the objective of the best New York press was—as Pulitzer demanded—to investigate to the bottom of things and to use narrative technique to capture attention. News had to be vivid. Enormous space could be dedicated to a seemingly minor item that was interesting to the man on the street. North American journalists considered themselves to be scientists or realist artists. They understood this to be not only the mimetic function of texts, but the identification of "reality" with external phenomena. José Martí, on the other hand, admirer of the *Herald*, moved away from the "externality" of descriptions in his chronicles to defend the "I" of the literary subject and the right to subjectivity. According to García Marruz, Martí learned his imaginative flight from Spanish Americans, the idea of a superior art and the gravity of the past from Europeans, but the efficacy of fact and the influx of life from United States journalism.[2]

Comparing Martí's chronicles from 1880 to 1892, when he was a correspondent in New York, to American texts that appeared in the press at that time helps us understand his writing.[3] Martí was a great reader of the New York press. He admired the *Herald*, for example, which had begun doing big covers and special editions dedicated to a single area of interest a half-century earlier. He contributed to the *Hour*, and especially to Charles Dana's *Sun*. Dana eventually wrote Martí's obituary.

The *Sun* was "the bridge between the older press and the new journalism that was to develop before the end of the century."[4] Like the biggest newspapers of the city, it aimed its editorials and writing style at workers, small businessmen, and immigrants. The lesson of the *Sun* was very important for Martí the chronicler: Dana's stated objective was to present as clearly as possible a daily photograph of the elements of the world. He created his newspaper with his writers, in simple and clear pages, so that it would also represent the people of New York. He showed interest in politics, economics, and government, but he maintained that first came "the people."[5] One of his biographers writes that "he had the indefinable newspaper instinct that knows when a tomcat on the steps of City Hall is more important than a crisis in the Balkans."[6]

This was the time of great editorial crusades, of war correspondents abroad, of sensationalist press. Martí, in New York, read and admired writer-journalists such as Mark Twain and Walt Whitman. He was swept off his feet by the detective-reporter of his two favorite newspapers, the *New York Tribune* and the *Evening Sun*, Jacob Riis. This Danish critic of the capitalist system wrote scandalous chronicles about the poor neighborhoods of New York. His defense of the lower classes enjoyed such success that they later reappeared in his book, *How the Other Half Lives* (1890).[7]

What could be better training for a literature such as modernism than to be "where things happen"? Modernism wanted to be capable of following the rhythm of change, to "reflect in itself the multiple and confused conditions of this time, condensed, not prosaic, courageous, and informed by supreme artistic genius" (XXI, 163). As Aníbal González put it: "The chronicle put the modernity of modernist writing to the test, and took literature to the limit of its abilities in order to inscribe the present moment" (96).

Even though the tone of the best North American journalism did not emphasize the narrator's position, as modernist chronicles did, "objectivity" in the nineteenth century was not a part of the specificity of discourse. Journalism had to take a side. It could not be neutral, even in the selection of news. The interest of local readers ruled. The Associated Press news agency found the need for objectivity. Its goal was to sell news to the whole country, and therefore it wanted to present it in the most "objective" (distant) light possible, in order to interest a wider public. Just at the tail end of the century the *New York Times* became successful by imposing a more "informative" model than had been used thus far, a model for narrating stories or reports.

In order to broaden the context of the Spanish American chronicle, we should note that Europe tended to editorialize more, whereas the United States gave preference to news. But these are only partial tendencies. The most modern press produced in the West was documentary journalism understood as narration, because "the facts would be there, but their point was as often to entertain as to inform."[8] What's more, the transfer of information was not the only talent of journalists. Both in the new profession of reporting and in the enthusiasm for telling stories, the facts were of less interest than popular writing and a personal style.

Martí particularly disliked realism in art because "it doesn't limit itself to copying what is bad: it exaggerates and invents greater evil. It does not present, along with evil, its immediate remedy: it falls into thinking that evil will be cured by presenting an exaggerated image of it." As a modernist, his goals were to achieve beauty and harmony and to find what is praiseworthy in the human being; yet he conceded to the realists that nothing is absolutely good or bad. If the realist school faithfully recorded social ills, it would be rational and just and would accomplish its good deed. However, this record should not be used to justify wrongs or to make a spectacle of open wounds, but to isolate and create antipathy toward the wrongs that occur and to discover how the blood that constantly flows from wretched beings can be stanched (VII, 26).

3. Introspection

In Martí's time the awareness of modernity suffuses everything. As established systems of perception begin to fall, the forms of expression will change as well. Journalism becomes the ideal medium through which to contact, day to day, the flow of a new society. It tries to know men. The writer questions the immediate and his subjectivity at the same time. The "I" and personal experience in some way replace science. Only what is subjectively lived seems secure. As Martí writes, "And where are we to begin studying, if not within ourselves? We must sink our hands into our innards and look at the blood in the sunlight. Otherwise, we cannot advance" (XX, 372–73).

It is precisely in this *immediacy* and in his peculiar way of understanding subjectivism that the gap between Martí's poetics and romantic poetics occurs. Romanticism is also cemented in the "I," the senses, and their relationship to Nature. Martí was a romantic in his yearning for absolutes and his faith in the future, but he was more moderate in the scope of his social and political beliefs. Furthermore, it was essential to him to start from his own experience: "These are slashes in my own entrails—my warriors—. Not one has come out of my mind re-heated, artificial, recomposed. Rather they are like tears that spring from my eyes and blood that bubbles out of a wound."[9] He ratifies the value of subjectivity in one of his letters about his book *Ismaelillo*.

Do not read this once, because it will seem too strange. Read it twice, so that you will forgive me. I have seen those wings, those jackals, those empty glasses, those armies. My mind has been a stage, and all these visions have been actors upon it. My job has been to copy. This doesn't have a single line of thought. So, how am I to be held responsible for images that come to me without my bidding them? I have done nothing more than put my visions into verse. These scenes have wounded me so badly that I am still surrounded by them, as if I had before me a vast dark space with great white birds flying in it. (VII, 271)

The "I" that Martí introduces as the answer to modernity and to the *fin de siècle* crisis is not confessional or personalized. It is an "I" that seeks to include the universe, a *collective* "I" that expresses not individuality, but the soul of the world. This means, as Borges said, "that to try to express oneself and to express life itself are one and the same thing."[10]

The rupture that this conception assumes is of supreme importance. Martí's poetics, whether in poetry or in journalism, is not mimesis, or catharsis, or totalizing rationalization, since his truth is only that of the interior. Reality is fragmented, and so will be his poetics. Secularization has broken down myths, but now the transcendent feeds on everyday material. The "I" organizes and associates these concrete images in a way that reflects the laws of Nature—where what seems contradictory and antagonistic is really not, since it has its own harmony—elevating everyday stories and journalistic news to an ontological dimension. "We lend an ear to everything. Thoughts no sooner germinate than they are loaded with flowers and fruit, jumping off the page, like subtle dust, into all minds. Railroads overcome the jungle; newspapers, the human jungle" (VII, 227).

4. The Rhetoric of the Sublime: Whitman and the Greats

Martí wanted to account for modernity. He maintained that writers are in the battle of the new times, that their obligation is to interrogate their interior and Nature, become part of its cycles and laws. They must awaken elevated thoughts in others, as well as the search for meaning that justifies each person, because "human life would be a disgusting and barbaric invention, if it were limited to life on earth" (VII, 236).

But Martí uses not only what is new. He wanted "to make people cry, sob, rebuke, punish, make tongues crackle, possessed by thought, like a saddle when a rider mounts it. That's what I understand by writing. Not to strike one chord, but all of them. Not to excel in the painting of an emotion, but in the art of awakening all of them" (Trópico, LXXIII, 133–34).

In order to achieve this Martí retains a device used by Spanish American romantics and *costumbrista* writers alike: the rhetoric of oratory.[11] His writing bears at once his passion for the sublime and the mark of the oratorical tradition.[12] In fact, newspapers—and many popular poems—were read aloud to the illiterate for much of the nineteenth century, a practice that writers and editors doubtless took into consideration. Whether recovering older strategies of representing the sublime or continuing the Spanish American tradition, Martí was clearly as active an orator as he was a journalist. Subjectivity, immediacy, analogy, chromatism, and synesthesia: all flowed among political discourse, chronicles, and poems in which each influenced, enriched, and infected the other with the new poetics. Enrique José Varona describes the writer-orator:

I will never forget my delight while Martí spoke. The cadence of his sentences, which lacked only rhyme to be poetry, rocked my soul like true music and with the proper effects of music. Meanwhile, there passed before me, like a swarm of golden bees, like spouts of luminous water, like flowers of fire unfolding in the heavens, handfuls of gold, sapphire, and emeralds, his sonorous words, in a wash of amazing images that seemed to rise in interminable spirals and fill space with the ghost of light.[13]

If oratory seems more pertinent to the nineteenth century than to the twentieth, Martí turned it into a different product with his syncretist style. So much so that its construction can be compared—as was noted earlier—in many cases with the work of the quite modern Walt Whitman, who also discovered the sublime in the secret interrelations among the living. Few chroniclers used oratory in all its richness; many limited themselves to addressing the reader, or to using maxims and exclamations. Martí enriches the textual system with his mixture of journalism, literature, and oratory. Furthermore, he gleans only what is useful from each technique, "because before rhetoric oppressed talent, talent created rhetoric" (Trópico, L, 50).

Martí's precision in handling oratory leads him to effects that create such an impression of liveliness that the characters—including the narrator—want to leave the page. As Miguel de Unamuno said, Martí's verses are life-giving and lifelike.[14] Martí worked with a strange mix of images and techniques that would form a new and fragmentary prose made of sensations selected and ordered by the narrative "I." In that moment of defining discursive spaces, Martí's work presents a new understanding of the creative potential of the act of reading. The moral character that Martí assigns writing differentiates him from the aesthetes and even from other modernists, while his impressionism, his symbolism, his Parnassianism, and his use of synesthesia distance him also from the romantics. At the same time, his perception of modernity led him to include the fragmentariness, impressionism, and speed that marked the literature of the early twentieth century. Yet his work differs from all these movements because it demonstrates a vigor that must be called moral: Martí's images tend to break the balance of the familiar, searching for new harmonies in elements that seem adverse. His practice coincides with the philosophies of Guyau, Tarde, and Fouillé, who believed the power of visual suggestion on thought to be a way of avoiding determinism and reclaiming free choice for man.[15] Since "intelligence is the power both to discern and to unite, then to think about exterior things is to entwine them, and science consists of this entwining . . . Within that limit, we can say, like the God of Boileau, 'I don't think about things to come only because they will occur, but they will occur in part because I think them'" (Fouillé, 277).

Martí believed in the improvement of man. He fought to achieve this by infecting his fellow man with images to break the mold in which his peception had fallen asleep. Along with Whitman, he said: "He who shows a wider chest juxtaposed with mine, shows the wideness of my own chest" (XIII, 140). For Longinus and for him, a single virtue was enough to overcome defects. Martí's modern search for beauty was not abstract, it was also moral. He reflected: "The beauty of form should envelop the good precept, as the height of the characters should envelop the good example" (Trópico, XL, 99). This is where the general balance lies in his *Escenas norteamericanas,* which so scrutinize and admire that society. He expresses this in his sketch of General Grant by way of two perfect decasyllabic lines with caesuras of six and seven syllables: "Guilty he may have been; but then his sin will always be much smaller than his greatness" (XIII, 43).

Martí wanted to communicate to the reader that he could find peace and stability in a dialogue with Nature. He wanted to infect the reader with the ecstasy that Plato talks about in *Phaedrus*: a godly pleasure that lends wings to the soul and is tied to beauty and reminiscence. It is what Longinus called the sublime: proportioned disproportion, the vehemence of emotions, the divine, that which overwhelms and amazes. It is that which assumes the duty of producing resonance, of impregnating souls and preparing them for noble sentiments.[16]

The North American chronicles contain devices of the old rhetoric of the sublime. This is Martí's typical move to connect disparate times, making the stylistic observations of Longinus, Fouillé, or Whitman flow into a point of intersection. To achieve this, he inserts his extraordinary analogies in constructions that tend to obey the rules of oratory: the sublime appears born of the orator himself. The descriptions of this type of experience in "Emerson," for example, do not cite Emerson, but begin with an unusual use of the impersonal pronoun "se," which includes the narrator. In his essays dedicated to great men, he breaks free of the role of journalist as the mere mediator of information to become another protagonist of the story: "Flags are at half mast along with our hearts: Peter Cooper is dead. What he leaves behind is a populace of children. I was not born of this land—and he never knew about me—and I love him as a father. Had I crossed his path I would have kissed his hand" (XIII, 48). Rarely does Martí dedicate a whole chronicle to a single topic; when he does, it is usually to honor and compose portraits of great people who have just died. These heroes are usually poet-philosophers, orator-priests, or politician-warriors. If the chronicle is about a writer, Martí goes so far as to mimic his style, especially in the pieces about Longfellow, Emerson, and Whitman. The voice of the chronicler/narrator becomes confused with that of the poet, to form a single voice, without any more transition than a quotation mark, or sometimes nothing at all. This is a technique borrowed from oratory, when the speaker suddenly assumes the first person as if he were the character.

Martí also uses maxims. Of Beecher, he says: "Where reason wanders, faith in the harmony of the Universe blooms" (XIII, 33). His figures are based on collective myths: the portraits of Wendell Phillips and Peter Cooper are constructed on the images of Christ; Emerson and Whitman resemble priests or biblical prophets; and politicians are epic heroes. Rhythmic cadence, so vital for oratory, is also crucial to the musicality of the new poetic prose: it combines passion and serenity, silences, successions of exclamations or questions, transpositions, and onomatopoeia. "Whitman," for example, features anaphora: the second paragraph alone repeats the word "man" eight times (XIII, 131). It contains apanalepsis: "sacred is sweat and the shroud is sacred" (XIII, 134). He includes silences indicated by blank spaces and punctuation, as well as parallel constructions such as beginning sentences with only slightly different variations: he makes himself, he reads, he doesn't live, he says, he is (XIII, 132–33). Another typical device in his chronicles is antinomy: "it is not . . . but."

The richness of Spanish assonance and alliteration stands out: "awakening in the fertile forests of the shore, those faded flowers and the nests. Pollen flies; beaks peck kisses; branches pair off" (XIII, 133). The succession of suggested images holds together by the association of contiguous ideas: flowers/nests/flying/pollen, beaks/kisses/pairing/branches. Here is another sample, in which the "o," "m," "n," and "s" sounds create a sense of flow, in conjunction with the rhythm of punctuation and groups of consonants and word repetition. It creates the impression of a stream though it is describing a cemetery: "a bone is a flower . . . Suffering is less for those souls whom love possesses; life has no pain for those who know its meaning in time" (XIII, 134).

Accumulations also appear, as well as internal consonance, transformed phonic sequences, and especially changing caesuras and enjambed final paragraphs:

To hear the songs of things, with palms open to the air. To surprise and proclaim gigantic fertilities with delight, gathering the seeds, battles, and orbs in Edic* verses. Signaling to the amazed times, the radiant hives of men stretch and rub the fibers of watchful liberty with their bee's wings, in the American valleys and peaks. They shepherd friendly centuries toward the peace of eternal calm, while their friends serve them the first catch of the spring sprinkled with champagne, on country cloths. (XIII, 142–43).

Martí wanted to create diverse pauses in the rhythm of the reading, which is why he resorted to nonacademic punctuation. His texts often include dashes as a sort of long comma—they indicate a greater pause in the reading than a regular comma. Colons reappear several times within the same sentence, not to indicate similarities or derivations, but as a way of slowing the rhythm of reading.[17]

The following are examples of Martí's rhetorical strategies, in accordance

*Translator's note: Martí uses the neologism "édico," from the Latin root *edere*, "to give birth."

with an oratory that pursues the sublime. This paragraph, expressionistic in style, includes strategies of the rhetoric of the sublime, such as gradation, accumulation, question and response, the change of persons, abundant metaphors, and periphrasis: "Do we still not know what his verses are? They are sometimes like a bearded old man, with a snake-like beard, tortuous hair and a bright gaze, leaning on an oak stick, like a gigantic angel with golden wings descended into the abyss from the green mountains on high. Marvelous old man, I leave at your feet my beam of light from fresh palms, and my silver sword!" (30).

The chronicle on the death of President Garfield is rich in rhetorical devices. It presents dramatizations, with dialogues of a past action narrated in the present. These representations are so vivid that the narrator seems like a protagonist or direct witness. Exaltations, apostrophied fury interspersed with pain, sentences that never reach their end, and the disappearance of conjunctions and verbs are all here:

The assassin does not even deserve for the price of the crime to be pinned on him. No! For turning our hands to Him, who sees us from his tomb with paternal eyes, must they be stained with vile blood and impiety? The evil jealous one rests in his cave, his darkness, his oblivion! May rock and iron accompany, until the final stages of his defamed life, his heart of rock and iron! Men who have to create themselves and deserve their heroes don't have time to kill an evil one! (206)

After the autopsy, the broken body closed, began the colossal apotheosis. This dead man has crossed the country on paths made of flowers, among sobs and wails, among prostrate crowds. He has gone through mourning armies, flags, festoons, cretonnes, and laurels. He has been offered gifts by monarchs and love by the people, glorious offerings. He has traveled on pillows of roses, under garlands of gold, through hallways of marble! (XIII, 207)

Exaltation is reinforced by verb successions such as "he loved, founded, consoled" (XIII, 49). It also is communicated through gradual accumulation: "he claimed his crime, begged his fear, the battles raged, and his victories spread their wings" (XIII, 34). He surprises the reader with unusual adjectives such as the "mosesque anger" of Emerson, and of unusual images such as the dust that becomes snow as it falls on Longfellow's coffin (XIII, 230).

5. Roots: "Calderón's Centennial"

Old and new come together in a conscious way in Martí's prose. This contagion of and by different times accords with his dualistic thinking regarding inside and outside, up and down, ancient and contemporary.

One of the tools valued by writers in the nineteenth century was philology, and the romantics had this very much in mind. Martí says in the prologue to "Poema del Niágara" that "there is no greater pleasure than that of knowing the origin of every word that is used, and what its scope is" (XIII, 234). But Martí was to place his own spin on language, distinct even from Emerson's model.[18] The search for the roots of language led Emerson to dig in the ancient Saxon for equivalent terms, in order to discard the Latinisms of his own language. Martí, on the other hand, resuscitated the technique of conceptualism from Spain's Golden Age. He did not limit himself to a few archaisms, but included the Góngora-style hyperbaton and the Calderón baroque style that stemmed similarly from everyday images as the analogy of a universal category. Martí also borrowed Baltasar Gracián's conceptual and lexical sharpness, including his sensitivity to the density of each word's meaning, as well as a tendency toward aphoristic sentences or those beginning with the impersonal reflexive pronoun "se." He especially developed a taste for creating new words based on existing ones. Martí's neologisms are many: airosity, scrupulate, stealor, snooper.[19]

Martí's attention to Renaissance conceptualism may have taught him some of the techniques used by the symbolists as well, such as the absurd comparison of elements that have no relation. Also in this category is the joining of internal and external figures, the transformation of one image into another, the use of contrast and paradox, antithesis, and the lexicon of sublimation. He also used the Quevedian device of using common words in a new sense—such as "peinar" (to comb) instead of "pasar" (to pass)—thus creating a new linguistic system based on the former one.

There are some articles by Martí, such as "El centenario de Calderón" (Calderón's Centennial), in which this appropriation of Renaissance devices takes shape in an obvious manner, since it fits the subject: the style of each of Martí's chronicles varies according to the internal demands of the topic at hand. "Calderón's Centennial" begins with an apothegm: "To honor the dead is to invigorate the living" (XV, 109). There are hyperboles such as "the most elevated poet who has rhymed in the vernacular" (109). Antitheses abound: rebel philosopher/gentle serf, king of his own/soldier of kings (111); pompous procession/humble party, graying men/jolly servants (112). Series of tricolor gradation also appear. Conceptualist diction abounds: "steeds of perfumed unction," "rebel mustaches" (109), "carriages that do not roll but moan" (111), "box of jewels," "human roses" (112). This text also contains hyperbolic transformations such as "Night of the tropics, breast of stars, bouquets of lights" (110), as well as terms that refer to Spain at that time (ingeniousness, cape passing, fame, Moorish styles). Some constructions open with a metaphor and modulate into the real image: "then come waves of gauze, with flowery foam—and they are the schoolgirls of Madrid . . . Innumerable winged worms follow—and they are the bright pennants carried by innumerable youngsters, the schoolboys of Madrid" (122). When Martí seems about to reuse a tired cliché, it is only to transform the expression into something new and startlingly different: "the silent remains that were once a prison to that eloquent soul" (110). Martí uses asceticism as a topic. He invents Latinate words freely and makes frequent reference to figures out of Golden Age drama, especially Don Juan. Martí also sprinkles the text with lines that mimic the rhythm of the *endecasílabo*, a traditional Spanish verse form which has eleven syllables per line: *"lindo es Madrid en todo el mes de mayo"* (Lovely is Madrid in all the month of May, 109), *"alfombra de cabezas son las calles"* (a carpet of heads are the streets), and *"y vieron luego las absortas calles"* (and then they saw the streets absorbed, 111). And of course, Martí uses hyperbaton: "those hybrid times in which from the hair of their ladies the gallants made braids for their hats."

6. The Universality of Local Lore

The obsession with modernity affected the poets of both Europe and the Americas. In response to a sense of destruction and genesis in their immediate environments, both groups opted for a poetics of universalism and the consequent break with regionalism.[20] The web of borrowings, concomitances, and transformations that cemented the new poetics becomes difficult to trace because recontextualizing and mixing techniques results in a poetics whose internal system of laws is distinct and autonomous. Martí learned everything he could, was attentive to any innovation and cultural novelty, but always preached that Spanish America must be firm "with the black trunk of fallen pines, as well as the wonderful branches of new pines: That's what we are! New pines!" (quoted in Vitier, 88).

The different results that curiosity produces in creators when they turn to etymology in order to clean out their language is notable: Emerson reached synthesis, and Martí the baroque.[21] Describing Martí's work as baroque may seem contradictory, since Martí repeatedly claimed: "The art of writing, isn't it to reduce? Verbosity certainly kills eloquence. There is so much to say that it must be said in the least number of words possible. Of course, every word must have wings and color" (XIII, 196). Although capable of describing complex situations in very little space, Martí sometimes launches into florescent prose that can seem overdone, hyperbolic. It must be read carefully in order to see that he does not inflate, and that there are no vacuous phrases. His expansions tend to lead to precision, and the breaks in the syntax also break the mechanics of reading, and therefore of perception. His baroquism is natural: there is no place for bejeweled writing in his lines, because, as he said in *Versos libres*, "my verses are scrambled and ignited / like my heart."[22]

Sanín Cano, whose universalism and awareness of modernity link him to the modernists, maintained that Stuart Mill's slogan, *nemeso apistein* (be sure to doubt), ought to reign in his time, "which can also be that of Renán and Taine."[23] This generalized doubt, the essence of the symbolists, may help to explain the rapid popularity and wide influence of impressionism, since learning to see reality with critical or skeptical eyes would suggest that the smooth, even deployment of color in traditional painting did not correspond to the processes of nature. Martí found affinities between his own art and impressionist painting, to which he dedicated quite a bit of attention as art critic for the North American press. Sanín Cano also dismissed the idea that each artistic movement must be isolated and autonomous. He claimed that the humanization of landscape was not exclusive to the impressionists, since the modern sense of nature could already be detected in Rousseau, Tasso, Fray Luis de León, or Virgil, making this kind of artistic genealogy no more than an "athletic exercise" (Sanín Cano, 20).

The challenge is to find a form of one's own, a style that is not mere imitation. The modernists' obsession is that of the new man, of discerning "the new altars, big and open like forests" (XIII, 225). Therefore, just as important as the borders between literary discourse and State or journalistic discourses, is the awareness of temporality. The development of modernism's new styles expresses the excitement of new blood. "Style, more than form, is in the personal conditions that have to express themselves through it . . . He who adjusts his thought to his form, like a sword to the scabbard, has his style. He who covers the scabbard with paper or golden string will not improve the temper of the blade" (V, 128).

Writing has to be like the times: although everything logical appears to be contradictory, in the text ideas must fit the consonants, the motion, the sound, and the tactile, auditory, and visual sensations. In order for such a match to occur, there must be an awareness of the origin and meaning of each word, without aspiring to formal perfection, which would end up sacrificing the force of the ideas. Nature is irregular, and force lies in irregularity. In the end, writing should produce the pride of a sculptor, a painter, a warrior: "Light is the supreme pleasure of men. It paints a river, sonorous, turbulent, tossing, broken into silver dust, evaporated into colored smoke. The stanzas are paintings: now a gust of wind, now columns of fire, now lightning. Now Luzbel, now Prometheus, now Icarus. *It is our time faced with our Nature*" (XIII, 233).

It is the sense of temporality in Martí's poetics that makes his work such a space of condensation: he effectively combines democracy and epic, Nature and social and intimate reality, the decadent pain of Parnassians and symbolists, the multiple life marching toward the future sung by Whitman, the discovery of cosmic harmony and economic liberalism, existential anxiety and criticism of injustice.

He wrote of Whitman:

He does not force comparison, and in fact does not compare. He tells what he sees or remembers with a graphic and incisive complement. He confidently possesses the impression of the ensemble that he sets out to create, and employs his art, which he hides entirely, to reproduce the elements of his canvas in the same disorder in which he observed them in nature . . . He sketches, but, let's say, with fire. In five lines he can gather, like a handful of gnawed bones, all the horrors of war. One adverb is enough to expand or contract a sentence, and one adjective enough to sublimate it. His method must be ample, since the effect is just that, but one could presume he has no method at all. (XIII, 142).

Contradictions come in contact with a formula of dialectic synthesis, if not a solution, in the texts constructed with this temporal understanding. They include impressionistic brushstrokes, a philological awareness of language, vital rhythm, a multitudinous vision, a nostalgia for past heroism and a desire for the future, as well as use of the symbol as insinuation. Images that could seem arbitrary reveal themselves at the end of the reading to be part of a structured system. Martí explains this writing method in his chronicle about Emerson: "Sometimes it seems that he jumps from one thing to another, and the connection between two immediate thoughts is not apparent at first. That which is a jump for others is a natural step for him. He moves from peak to peak, like a giant . . . His thoughts seem isolated, but he sees so much at once and wants to say it all, just the way he sees it" (XIII, 22).

His discussion of Whitman reveals much of Martí's own poetics:

He mixes [words] with unprecedented audacity, juxtaposing the august and almost divine with others that pass for less appropriate and decent. Some pictures are not made of epithets, which in his case are always lively and profound, but of sounds . . . His caesura, unexpected and galloping, changes incessantly . . . To accumulate seems to him the best way to describe. His reasoning never takes the pedestrian forms of argument or the haughty forms of oratory. Rather it has the mystery of insinuation, the fervor of certainty, and the ignited turn of prophesy. At every step in his books are these words of ours: *viva, comrade, liberty, Americans.* (XIII, 141–42, emphasis Martí's)

If we add to these "words of ours" the words *eagle, blue,* or *mountain,* for example, couldn't the same description be applied to the North American chronicles of José Martí? Is not this indistinct flow of creation from one genre to another the poetics of Martí's verses? Martí is not a literary offspring of Whitman's, but reading *Leaves of Grass* helped him to ratify and perfect his own aesthetic.[24] The text about Whitman is from 1892, the last phase of Martí's work as a correspondent. Here he combines analogy, liberty of rhythm, lexicon, and syntax, resulting in chromatism, synesthesia, musicality, multiplicity, and symbolism. Carried out this way, journalism was not the soporific cliché that Manuel González Prada described.[25]

Whether or not Martí fulfilled his ambition, awareness of temporality produces another schism in his texts: his faith in the future mixed up the order of events, an order anchored in patterns of causality by Darwinism, Spencerism, and even Krausism, with their "critical harmonizations" (Vitier, 132). His writing tends to overturn the chronological order of events or ideas, or the facts are laid out backwards. The effect appears before the cause. As Claude Bochet-Huré observes: "It was natural that this tendency to invert the logical expression of mental steps should also be reflected in the order of terms in the interior of sentences. . . . It is clear that Martí's pen and his thinking take charge first and foremost of what he deems essential: the result of facts, and the conclusion of ideas."[26]

7. Writing as Artifice

The Western worldview has become secularized. Crowds are an everyday experience, and a new religion resides in each person as "the voice of the unknown . . . a more or less complete copy of the world we live in" (XIII, 220). Nature is "the magician who unfolds her wordless answers." With Nature as their inspiration—as Martí said, "the same magician kissed everyone"—the new poets of the city create symbolic images that suggest the hidden meaning and universal harmony behind the imbalance of society. José Martí says in his commentary on Pérez Bonalde's style that Nature for the new poets is no longer the romantic landscape that reflected emotional states as "dinner table confessions" (235). There are personal and intimate poets who pour only their moaning into Nature, while those who are healthy and vigorous are able to find in Nature a new philosophy. This, he announces, "is merely the secret of the relations of various forms of existence" (232). The poet must unveil it.

Martí's chronicles enter into problematic tension with their era. Traditional systems of representation are of no use to this model of perception. The mimetic image has lost its meaning, and there is no certainty in the veracity of an appearance. Another system of representation needs to be established, in which the secret—the relationship between various forms of existence—can be intuited. The image, then, cannot pretend to be more than a technique, a construct, an interpretation. It is an artifice that relates more universal matters with the everyday. It is a mysterious and ambivalent symbol.

Art no longer imitates life; it recreates it, in its own order, ambiguously and no less authentically. In Martí's chronicles and poems, Nature is no longer what it was to the romantics: a landscape projected out of the soul of the protagonist in order to represent his varying emotional state. Nor is it a geographic determinism that conditions human beings from their birth. On the contrary, Martí's allusions to Nature are purely symbolic, as in the text of Emerson. Emerson is represented in the text as an eagle and a young pine, with a forehead like a mountainside, as well as a voice made of luminous clouds (XIII, 18–19).

Everything has become blurred, including order, laws, and institutions. Man occupies the place of the creator—if he is fully a man—and carries out his first duty, to create. As Martí says in his homage to Emerson: "He felt himself a man, and Godly for being so" (XIII, 20). Creating means a permanent aperture, tumult and pain. This system of representation—that of analogy—barely manifests the yearning to reunite all that seems disjointed, to reconstruct some sort of balance through images. This was not Martí's only system, as we shall see. The symbol invokes a hidden meaning in every object.[27] In a time when everything seems contradictory, the symbol does not resolve antagonisms, but forms a space of condensation or synthesis.

Martí does not use the term "artifice" for this technique of perception and writing. But although it seems paradoxical, the symbolic technique presupposes that the image is always a construct of the human mind: an element of nature becomes a symbol only under the gaze that selects it. This artifice could be more truthful than mimesis.

Martí adopted liberal views, especially in trying to fight commercial protectionism (cf. IX, 375–86). But this is very different from adhering to what he called "the timorous positivist doctrine, which in its healthy desire to distance men from idle mental constructions ends up stopping humanity in its tracks . . . The human journey consists of reaching the country that is described within us, which a constant voice is promising" (XV, 403).

He was not the only one to attack a philosohy that recommended knowing only that which is visible, or, in the case of art, representing objects only as they are. Gutiérrez Nájera said: "If the principle of art were imitation, the ultimate goal would be the complete illusion of the senses. If such an illusion were required, then the most sublime artist would be the mirror that most faithfully represented objects. Monstrous error!"[28] The Colombian Sanín Cano, one of the most informed and committed critics of Spanish American literature of the end of the century, was convinced of the need to liberate language from antiquated features, and defended the ideas of symbolism and impressionism. In his articles, he attacked what he called Zola's lack of culture and metaphysical incapacity: "Do we know what the real world is like? . . . In judging ourselves, we give but a distorted image of ourselves. In representing objects, we can only offer approximate images, necessarily carrying the stamp of our personal temperament."[29]

The break was clear to Sanín Cano: what mattered about art was making something beautiful—as he put it—without imitating everything in Nature.

His goals were to unite distinct planes, the high and the low, the cosmic and the banal, life and death, what seems contradictory or dual, the external and the internal, as José Martí understood: "What I can touch is called tangible. The study of the tangible world is called physics. The study of the intangible world is called metaphysics. The exaggeration of the first school is called materialism, and the exaggeration of the second is known as spiritualism, although it should not be called by that name. Both units are the truth" (Vitier, 126). The issue was to relate concepts and images in order to *signify*. Therefore descriptions or enunciations as simple or concrete as "sincere man" or "palm" weave together in the textual fabric in such a way that they refer to a suprareal dimension, passing through an ordering "I." This is the case with Martí's famous lines, "I am a sincere man / from where palms grow / I come from everywhere / And everywhere I go. / I am art among the arts. / In the mountains I am a mountain" (*Versos sencillos*). *The image is impossible within the referential order*, but in the text it synthesizes, describes, suggests a sentiment with no need for arguments or reasons. It condenses a meaning with an inexplicable force.

Examples of this crop up everywhere in the North American chronicles, where classic *imitatio* of art has been replaced with the autonomy of expression: cities are ovens, islands are baskets, and steam engines are white ants that talk by crossing their antennae ("Brooklyn Bridge," IX, 431). The Ohio River is a herd of colts that "speed" with winged helmets, and the entire earth spins with the dice on New York gaming tables ("Las inundaciones de Ohio" [The floods of Ohio], IX, 353). A speech becomes vengeful images that emerge from portraits on the wall, or a rain of burning stones ("Wendell Phillips," XIII, 64). A house fire is red eagles illuminated in their crests and strips of clouds scratching the earth, while eyes become empty nests ("Garfield," XIII, 200, 208). Barbaric armies of urban multitudes are stone warriors with gold helmets and shields and red lances ("Emerson," XIII, 17). Images of different orders appear in a succession that is impossible outside of written speech, as in the following description of an orator:

The pro-slavers' swords would have been mortified that night, had they been stripped of their *clothing*. There was a burning wave eating at their feet, reaching their knees and jumping up to their faces. It was an enormous fault, a tooth-filled jaw, that opened at its base. It was like an elegant wand of light that turned into wings. It was as if a celestial giant was ripping off slices of hillsides and throwing them on the evil people. (XIII, 58)

Some of the images cited here fit into neither symbolism, nor the subjective pulse of impressionism, nor the plasticity of Parnassianism. They are more akin to expressionism, even though that European movement was still in its embryonic stages at the time of Martí's death.[30] Sometimes emotion, fantasy, and synesthesia are the forces behind Martí's jump to expressionism. The expressionist image represents an object not for one of its real qualities, but for the impression it produces. There are examples of this in many of the *Escenas norteamericanas*: "Frightful birds, ignored by other men, seem to have attached themselves to their skulls, pecking at them, and flagellating their backs with their furiously crazed wings," he writes in "Terremoto de Charleston" (Charleston earthquake) (XI, 68). On another occasion he attacks Chicago anarchists' recourse to violence:

Bone-colored circles show,—when these lessons are read—, in a sea of smoke: a phantom enters a room full of shadows, gnaws on a human rib and files his nails. To measure the depths of human desperation, it is necessary to see whether fright, which usually keeps one prepared in times of calm, overcomes that which rises, indignant, with the fury of centuries. It is necessary to live exiled from homeland or humanity. (XI, 339–40)[31]

He says of the language of Walt Whitman that it resembles "the storefront of a butcher-shop, hung with animals; other times it is like the chant of patriarchs seated in a chorus, with the gentle sadness of the world at the hour when smoke disappears into the clouds. Other times it sounds like a brusque kiss, like something forced, like the cracking of dried leather that bursts in the sun . . ." (XIII, 141). Art does not imitate life, according to Martí, it constructs another reality: "Art is nothing more than manmade Nature . . . Nature gives man her objects, which are reflected in his mind, which in turn governs his speech, in which each object will turn into a sound" (XIII, 25).

One can conclude, for example, that the symbol as system of representation had already been discovered by the Europeans. The awareness of modernity was common in more than one hemisphere. The numerous points where Martí's thinking is aligned with the symbolists in general, as well as with another writer passionate about modernity, Arthur Rimbaud, seem more than coincidences. Rimbaud too replaced romantic subjectivism with a more "objective" subjectivism, taking knowledge of his own being as a reference point for understanding the universal. Rimbaud also derived "the radiant birth of his visions" from suffering (Rama, "La dialéctica," 196).[32] The French symbolists had resorted to a similar strategy: images no longer represented a specific idea for them; rather they tried to translate thought into images that grouped heterogeneous objects and actions. These images referred to each other in order to insinuate an explanation of the unknown through the familiar, or to suggest a state of mind. Furthermore, the symbolists subordinated the logical and grammatical structures of language to metaphoric forms. Like them, Martí did not presume to have invented the symbol. He was, like the symbolists, intuitive, visionary, representative, but less mystic and more traditional: the polarity expressed in his symbolic language—which often resolves itself—is inherited from the romanticism and positivism of the nineteenth century.

8. Musicality

It is difficult to know if the artistic changes and innovations of the late nineteenth century were brought about by the increased flow of information among countries or developed autonomously in response to modernization in each specific locale. We would have to turn to very different sources in order to answer that question. For our purposes, it does not matter which country first produced a particular element or if Martí, for example, discovered Parnassian geometric prose through Emerson or came to it on his own, thanks to his zeal for finding the exact term for each emotion. At age twenty-two, Martí began making his first notes on the possibility of enriching expression with sound effects and the musical arts. He wanted to incorporate the deep and languid echoes that become lost in space, as well as the tenacious rhythm that was so close to poetry, which "is more beautiful for what one wishes it to be than for what it actually is" (Trópico, I, 23–24). His early enthusiasm for the techniques of literary composition aimed to express the elusive: intuition displaces the concept from a word or phrase in order to make room for connotation and the phonic aspect.

The so-called Spanish American romantics, such as Esteban Echeverría, thought that poetry was in the idea. Domingo F. Sarmiento, who was also concerned with form, agreed with that concept: "The Latin American writer must sacrifice the author in favor of the advancement of his country, and self-esteem in favor of patriotism."[33] Martí attacked Parnassians and proponents of pure art for their attraction to vacuous beauty. But he believed, like the modernists, that poetry is not only in the idea, and that music, an emotion, or a vision can also spark understanding beyond concrete knowledge.[34]

If we compare dates, we can conclude that Martí was ahead of Paul Verlaine in formulating the theory of musicality as a writing device. Verlaine had published poems that experimented with these principles by 1875, but he did not systematize them as his "Art poétique" until 1884, in his book *Jadis et Naguère*.[35] Nevertheless, as Ned Davidson observes, Swedenborg's theories of "correspondence" between cosmic harmony and the human soul had planted the possibility of incorporating musicality into writing considerably earlier.

The idea was to learn from musical composition the techniques used to develop melody as a combination of peaks, timbres, pauses, and rhythms. This was supposed to lead to more subtlety and precision when expressing the elusive realities of the psyche. Davidson notes: "This intentional vagueness, was, in fact, an attempt to free poetry from the limitations of logical or conceptual expression, an attempt to make expressible the ineffable, through analogy and symbol. This was accomplished by the subordination of the denotative element of language and by the exploitation of its connotative power."[36]

The modernists began these experiments in Spanish America, although the effort to reproduce musical effects through phonic structures was more aptly metaphoric: sound cannot be transferred to physical space. But beyond metaphor, the connotation seems to ring true. Walter Ong observes: "All verbalization, including all literature, is radically a cry, a *sound emitted from the interior of a person* . . . The cry which strikes our ear, even the animal cry, is consequently a sign of an interior condition."[37] This cry of life, or this reproduction of breath turned into conscious writing, can notably increase the power of a text. An excellent example is "El terremoto de Charleston" (The Charleston earthquake), in which the rhythm of breaths and the repetition of sounds create a synesthetic representation of the catastrophe and the chanting of the blacks.

9. Fusion

It is perhaps better to talk about affinities than about influences. As Harold Bloom wrote: "Every young man's heart is a graveyard in which are inscribed the names of a thousand dead artists, but whose only actual denizens are a few mighty, often antagonistic ghosts."[38] It would probably be unjust or inaccurate to attribute the theory of musicality in writing exclusively to either Verlaine or Martí. Even geniuses do not generate themselves. For one individual to produce a masterpiece, many others must have been weaving a framework that prepares for that work and makes it possible. Only a select few will know how to mold and fit together the material successfully. Genius lies in this accomplishment. Martí himself wrote: "The only kind of writer who will be immortal in Latin America is the one who, like a Dante, a Luther, a Shakespeare, or a Cervantes of Americans, reflects the multiple and confused conditions of our time, condensed, unprosaic, stripped to the marrow, and informed by supreme artistic genius" (XXI, 163–64). The originality and novelty of the Dante to come are a clear combination in Martí's view: it is "tempering, supreme mastery" (XXI, 164). This is *poetic syncretism*. It is conciliation, or, as the Greek origin of the word indicates, the system which works to coordinate opposite parties or ideas. This is writing that, without betraying itself, makes the gesture of appropriating different realities to produce new modes of relation.[39]

José Martí's pan-American vision was also qualified by the necessities of universality and transculturation. His insistence upon using Nature as a frame of reference was more complicated than the logic of regionalism or determinism, both of which see individuals as products "molded" by their particular environments. Martí believed that one should write only about what one knew personally; this was one of the conditions of honesty. He found it false to write in the Caribbean using Scandanavian landscapes or colors, for example; but on the other hand he would have disagreed with the notion that the Americas' colors were singular or even permanent. He sharply disagreed with contemporary prejudices regarding geography and the predestination of the races.[40] For him, true genius was "to fraternize" "with the charity of one's heart and the daring spirit of the founders, with a headband and a robe."

This detail is not diminished because to assume the *mestizo* condition of Latin America is a step similar to the one that leads him to universalism. To fraternize is to return dignity to the black man, the Indian, and the peasant. It is accepting that there is a Spanish heritage, taking what is useful from other cultures, and always giving priority to their own history over that of others. What is essential is to ask questions, not to repeat: to know oneself.

Tired of useless hatred, of the resistance of books against spears, of reason against chaos, of the city against the country, of the impossible empire of urban casts divided about the natural nation, tempestuous or inert, there begins, unawares, the attempt at love. Populations stand up and greet each other. "What are we like?" they ask. And they tell each other what they are like . . . The frock coats are still French, but the thinking is beginning to be American . . . Creation is the password of this generation. (*Nuestra América*, 30)

This is the thesis of "Nuestra América" (Our America), which radiates throughout his work: to know and to make oneself known is the key to being free, because it is imperative to choose with lucidity and not in ignorance. This is Martí's way of fighting determinist rigidity.

Martí sums it up in *Versos sencillos:* "I come from everywhere and everywhere I go." The universalism of his poetics thus breaks with the traditions of romantic and *costumbrista* writing in Spanish America. It also breaks with the theories of many of his contemporaries. Lucio V. Mansilla, to cite one example among the chroniclers in the Argentine press of the time, dedicated a column to Emerson's sentence, "ice contains much study or much civilization."[41] His comments are pure irony aimed at the *yankee* "of that extravagant and fatalistic school of those who believe in the predestination of races." But the text's objective is to show the agility of creativity and humor: in the end it shares the ideology contained in Emerson's phrase.

Breaking away from imposed conventions does not mean searching for originality per se, nor does it mean committing literary parricide.[42] Martí believed that "Literary works are like children: they remake their parents" (XXI, 165), and "all human progress consists perhaps in returning to the point of departure"

(XXI, 226). He did not disregard heritage, but he concentrated on the rediscovery of man's spontaneity and nature, unmuzzled by foreign masks.[43] He says in the prologue to the poem by Pérez Bonalde that the parameters of germination from a fertile land are left behind, in the railroads that knock down jungles, ideas that are formed while moving, squares, cities, and newspapers. This leads him to rediscover the roots of things, what is still virgin and direct, not only in Nature, but even in useful images from biblical and Greek mythologies. José Martí wants to find a new lyricism that is also epic.

10. Between Realism and Redemption

Realism as a form of comprehension and expression maintained that truth is in the external. The modernists, on the other hand, looked for truth in the analogies among individual psychology, social existence, and Nature. The fictionalization of history in the modernist chronicles stemmed from this notion of truth, and not only from the writers' tendency to distinguish literature from journalism.

The next chapter will consider in more depth Martí's relationship with the North American press during his time as a correspondent in New York. It is useful, however, to keep in mind that he was not able to distance himself from the struggle between realists and idealists that took place in New York's intellectual arena. He had already written more than one piece of literary criticism against Zola's realism and naturalism, but he was forced to rethink his defense of subjectivism in the face of the major disputes between these two tendencies (VI, 324–26).

In addition to their effort to modify inherited concepts of man's relationship to Nature, the modernists struggled to reformulate the meaning of the material and ideal dimensions. For the modernists, material reality was deceptive and idealism insufficient. The spaces of condensation Martí established searched for transcendentalism in social life. He insisted upon writing that was *useful* for the betterment of mankind. His concern was to preserve the specificity of events and at the same time to discover their transcendent meaning. This purpose gave his work a quasi-religious character reminiscent of the European romantic historians. Like them, he considered writing an almost priestly activity, prophetic, and redemptive.[44] It is perhaps for this last purpose, redemption, that the image of Christ so often recurs in Martí's texts. It is not, however, the institutionalized or hagiographic Christ. As in all of his writing, images are analogies and symbols: a mountain is a forehead; gold represents not money but its opposite, purity; eagles are not birds of prey but signs of peace; and Christ does not allude necessarily to the system of Catholic beliefs, but to the many men who forgive, captivate, and love.

The symbology of Christ is developed this way in the prologue to "Poema del Niágara": "He is returning to Christ, to the crucified Christ, forgiving, endearing, with naked feet and open arms, not to a nefarious, satanic Christ, malevolent, hateful, angry, scolding, judgmental, and impious" (VII, 226).

Human redemption is Martí's way of responding to the sense of general crisis. The same reaction took place throughout the Western world in a Christian-pagan syncretism that was opposed to the "dominant logos."[45] In the same year in which the prologue to "Poema del Niágara" appeared, Ernest Renan published *Vie de Jesus*, an interpretation of the contemporary resurgence of the image of Christ and of its similarity to the image of Don Quijote. Renan wrote, "He is a perfect idealist: for him matter is no more than the sign of an idea, and what is real is a living expression of that which we do not see."[46]

Martí's poetics are not wholly romantic. Despite many romantic tendencies, the awareness of temporality in his work marks a different understanding of idealism. For Martí, romantic theories of poetic genius are not enough to discover spaces of condensation. Martí's idealism relies heavily upon the real and upon an organizing I around which history also gravitates. He wrote: "poetry must have its root in the earth and a basis of true facts" (XII, 185). Martí's idealism required that his texts create a new space and a new system of perception whose medium turned out to be the newspaper chronicle.

11. A New Genre

Techniques such as the *poeticization of the real* are part of the modernist chronicle's "literariness" and condition of poetic prose. The new poetics also led to the formulation of a new literary genre, if genre is understood as a way of conceptualizing reality, a mode of both internal and external orientation and composition, which in this case oscillates between literary and journalistic discourses in order to form its own space.[47] Structuralist indices such as the temporal and spatial orders of discourse corroborate the idea that Martí's chronicles constitute a new literary genre. These texts are—as journalism—a representative discourse dependent on the temporal dimension (like history or biography), but they glean devices such as fictionalization, analogy, and symbolism from literature. These devices create a space distinct from the referential: its propositions—as in lyric poetry—are neither rational nor temporal, but rather follow a logic of similarity or dissimilarity.

Martí's chronicles mix referential representation with the creation of an order that exists only in the space of the text itself. Further along we will examine Martí's account of the inauguration of the Brooklyn Bridge in order to see how its referential content—abundant in details about engineering—is intermingled with images of that same technology best described as hallucinatory.

Though they represent or express something real, these images constructed through a system of analogy create an order that is possible only within the text. The chronicle, which has undeniable referential value, is at once centripetal and centrifugal in its effect. Its linguistic signs operate as denomination and context (signification), while at the same time losing transparency in order to gain specific and independent weight, as in poetry.

Duality, the oscillation between genres and spheres, is characteristic of this new writing, which is neither poetry nor journalism in their conventional forms. This literature is—like the times of splendid elaboration that Martí talks about—a product in the process of creation and crisis. In most cases it was more a transition than a finished or balanced accomplishment, but in this position between one state and another the chronicle became a literary genre in its own right.[48]

The new genre chooses its topics among contemporary issues, especially those related to the city, international politics, culture, new discoveries, and great events. They are a sort of archeology of the cosmopolitan present. As a text that appears in newspapers, it must present a comprehensible and attractive coherence for the reader. It must be relevant, and not close in on itself, as supposedly happens with poetry. The modernist chronicle implies an ambiguous but usually critical posture toward institutional power and the bourgeoisie. This is a way of rebuilding on a daily basis a reality that had become fragmented. The style mixes resources to achieve an expression of each idea in images. It is careful with form and weighs its words, incorporating and even accentuating, when necessary, neologisms, nativisms, archaisms, and quotations in other languages.

The modernist chronicle first submits itself to the test of personal experience. It includes Nature, and makes its cultural allusions explicit. It is the muse-museum: since it is a literature that is born to break with convention, the only way of not becoming entangled in the web of self-readings is to verbalize them, show them, turn them into part of the setting that constructs the new perception.[49] Chronicle relies on the stylization of the literary subject. Unlike journalism, its narrative strategy is not objectivity. Even with the important element of referentiality, these texts tend to be heavily self-referential, often including reflections on the activity of writing itself.

This way of writing is one of the elements that defines the novelty of this genre, if by novelty we understand that which is not a repetition of schemes, figures, or meanings, that which surpasses "its epoch, its language, and the social institution in which and for which it was born" (Castoriardis, 18–19).[50]

Chapter 5

The Years in North America
Creating Local Lore from Abroad

I. Exile

Martí's *Escenas norteamericanas* invert the customary gaze: *he is the Other*, the small colonial subject, immersed in "the monster's entrails." He writes from marginality as a Cuban confronted by the metropolitan center, exiled in a city not his own, surrounded by a language foreign to him. The locus of power is displaced in his chronicles: the gaze focuses on New York (a familiar, yet threatening entity) rather than on the immediate colonial authority that Spain represented for Cuba.

Both admiring and critical of the society he describes, Martí maneuvers to reformulate the traditional use of "us" and "them," or better still, to construct for his use an inclusive Spanish American "Us." The poem "Amor de ciudad grande" (Love of a big city) begins with the line "The city appalls me!" and adds: "Yes, I am thirsty, but for a vintage which on Earth / Must not be tasted! . . . Go on and drink, you ruinous wine tasters / of paltry human wines . . . Drink! I am an honest man, and I am afraid!"[1] Terror and love, thirst for meaning and harmony, disappointment at the mercantile values of an ever more Darwinian society, fear, a sense of honor, and contempt: these are the vertices of modernity, but they indicate also the complex positioning of the writer's gaze, constructed *from* and yet *toward* the metropolis.

The location of the writer's gaze is not a mere detail. It defines not only the exile and the writing, but also the context of the gaze that produces this writing. The *Escenas norteamericanas* are at once the product of a society still subjected to colonialism and the agent of a national project. They are the direct witness of the Gilded Age and of North American imperialism. Martí's North American chronicles allow, among other things, the exploration of the relationship between the gaze and colonialist discourse, an investigation that is usually conceived from the site of enunciation of the colonizer. Homi Bhabha describes the gaze that is projected on the Other as one that describes the lack of the Other, who is colonized or barbaric according to the hegemonic culture's assumptions.[2]

In Martí's chronicles, however, the gaze does not rationalize the marginalized or colonized subject. Rather it positions itself in the site of Power. With

84

the terms of the game thus inverted, several problems arise. Martí's chronicles, seen as a writing of exile, suffer from a sense of displacement and yearn to create place. Generally, this type of writing translates the experience of a new place, which is identifiable even in its physical characteristics, and demands a language able to translate Otherness itself.[3] The confrontation with the Other—in this case not the marginalized or the colonized Other but the site of Power—allows a redefinition of one's identity by means of differentiation, as in Lacan's mirror stage (in recognizing the reflected image by what is different about it: "one's own wine" is recovered).[4]

2. Rebuilding a Place

Exile is the loss of home, of the ontological myth of reconciliation of time and space, the place of residence Bachelard described as brimming with metaphoric qualities.[5] A strategy for recovering this loss in the "Escenas norteamericanas" consists of using a national language, a brand of Spanish designed for the whole of Spanish America, as if to make the continent a coherent linguistic space. Thus, for Martí, language would be the agent of communal intelligibility, with a clear aim: to recreate the "us" of Spanish America by means of journalism. Home and identity are affirmed by creating a metaphor of "us" and "them." Writing is also an allegory of otherness itself. Martí wrote about this dichotomy in his notebook as early as 1871, at the beginning of his exile. The United States ("them," but at the same time "here") is the empire of the practical, of calculation, prosperity, and corruption. "Us," on the other hand, is the territory of the heart, of imagination and the new (XXI, 15–16). (Martí's global perspective on identity generally ignores the marked differences among Spanish American nations and politics.) This dichotomy undergoes further refinements until it becomes the fabric of one of his best known texts, "Nuestra América" (Our America) (1891). Here Martí is already able to warn about the threat of North American expansionism (represented in the well-known image of the "seven-league-giant"), to proclaim the individual existence of the two Americas, and above all, to sit as an equal at the continental table.

3. Identity and Language

If language, in exile, acquires the power of territory and location, then this writing—much more so than that of any other modernist author—significantly recovers its origin in the conceptualism of the Golden Age, as we discussed in the previous chapter. The return to conceptualism is a deliberate act of aesthetic definition that affirms common cultural identity for the hemisphere. On one hand it is a reconciliation with the Spanish heritage, and, on the other, as he established in his "Prólogo al Poema del Niágara de Pérez Bonalde" (1882), it is the construction of a writing that is "our time, faced with our Nature" (VII, 233). It is the creation of a literary system capable of authentically apprehending the present.

The chronicles contain some words in English. This fact should not be associated only with modernist cosmopolitan attitudes and notions of verisimilitude; it is also a sort of co-language. The use of untranslated words serves as a sign of intersection and a way of foregrounding cultural differences (Ashcroft, 66). The English used is mostly proper names: street names, cities, products, people, or magazine titles. On the rare occasions when he uses English nouns, he emphasizes them by using quotation marks or modifying the typography (for example: "ponie" or *lunch*).

Martí plays with the effect of reading the co-language. In order to evoke the exuberant productivity of the "Grand Livestock Exhibition" (1887), he mixes names of famous millionaires such as Vanderbilt, Pierpont Morgan, Le Grand B. Cannon, Appleton, Sloan, Tselin, and Douglas, with the breeds of cattle such as Jersey, Devon, Holstein, Hereford, and Lancashire, and these with the names of inventions used to make butter, to air milk, or to cure, such as "Stoddard," "Soper," "Vet," and "Lion." Swept along by enthusiasm, as is often the case, he introduces comments that seem to have come straight from the conflict between artificial men and natural men in "Nuestra América" (1891). Thus, at the end of the chronicle on the cattle show, he notes the eloquence with which people talk about "how in these doings of the milk universe, man grows up natural and good, and better than in any other business."[6]

In texts such as "Coney Island" (1881), he uses the names of beaches as a sort of magic rosary that adds detail as it distances the reader: *Manhattan Beach, Rockaway, Brighton, Gable* (134), or the "Agricultural building" (135). This already classic text combines Martí's exaltation of the prosperity of the United States with his fear of the feverish rhythm of its multitudes. In it we find one of Martí's most lapidary sentences: "those people eat quantity; we, class" (139). It is the beginning of his exile in New York, and the current of Martí's writing clearly verbalizes his sense of territorialization and borders: his logic is us-and-them rather than I-as-the-Other. Yet even amid the general enthusiasm of the chronicle, one senses the distress of the poem "Amor de ciudad grande": "It is well known that a melancholy sadness takes hold of the people of Spanish America who are living there [in the United States] . . . that no matter how much first impressions have flattered their senses, enamoured their eyes, dazzled and impaired their reason, . . . they feel like sheep with neither a mother nor a shepherd . . . because that vast land yonder is devoid of spirit" (138).

In his "Carta a Bartolomé Mitre y Vedia" (Letter to Bartolomé Mitre y Vedia) (December 19, 1882, [IX 15–18]), written at the beginning of his collaboration with *La Nación* of Buenos Aires, Martí calls a previous letter from the editor a "ray *from my own sun*": "I don't seem to be writing to a new acquaintance, but to an old friend, warm-hearted and high-minded." He makes a clear distinction between "our America" (Spanish America) and "here" (the United States). "Here" is the realm of "exclusive, vehement, and anxious love of material fortune," versus "the younger and more generously uneasy lands of our America." Martí erects his homeland upon this model, by engaging Spanish America in a dialogue whose subject is the metropolis. Martí's "here" is both temporal and other; it is regarded with the curiosity of one discovering modernity: the reification of goods, the creation of a new public space, confrontations with multiple and strange beings, experiences of displacement and disunity; all characteristics of the experience of exile as well. Writing chronicles was a way to earn a living—as the modernists often complained—but it was also a way to give form to that exilic experience, to witness, to produce a sort of revelation and recreate a native country (or Spanish America as a cohesive unit) for the reader by way of memory and writing.

4. Fact and Representation: Jesse James

In the chronicle "Jesse James, gran bandido" (Jesse James, the great bandit) Martí communicates the essential facts of James's assassination by mercenaries but shifts the text's focus from referentiality or reporting onto myth-making.[7]

On April 4, 1882, the front pages of both the *Sun* and the *New York Times* contained stories describing the details of James's death. In each the headline, summary, and newsy first paragraph are followed by a fictionalized but realistic *mise en scène* of the murder. In general, the articles these two newspapers published on this topic during the rest of the month emphasized the delinquent's noble physiognomy, his loving relationship with his wife, and the obtuse nature of the friends who killed him. From the masses' excitement and incredulity at the news and the mediocrity of the assassins, Martí extracts a saga that foregoes precise details but makes "Jesse James, gran bandido" a story cut in the spirit of the Renaissance and set in the Deep South of the United States. James becomes a knight of La Mancha like Don Quijote. The author repeatedly censures the bandit's violence, but manages to turn the episode into an ode to the beauty of the brave, beaten down by mediocre people who move in the shadows, whose implicit comparison to Judas is inevitable.

Although the beginning of Martí's text reflects the geography and North American context with allusions to New York, Missouri, and Kansas, another reality seeps in and permeates the tale: Martí invokes the Duke of Alba, Pizarro, and Flanders and builds toward the exaltation of bravery that diminishes the bumbling judges. He incorporates the motifs of the gentleman robber, the bullfight, the reddened ring, the ladies of Spain who throw their fans in the air, matadors, and Spanish *mantillas*, or shawls. These cultural associations extrapolate a simple and ephemeral piece of local news into the sphere of literary epic. Martí's unusual comparisons facilitate the leaps between spheres: he compares, for example, the serenity of a man cracking another's head with a bullet with that of a squirrel breaking open a nut.

The result is a chronicle that does not remove the reader from the dimension of reality and facts—as fantastic literature could—but rather introduces into that plane of reality a mode of perception that mythologizes and transcendentalizes it, without losing the equilibrium of the referential. It is a perfect example of the chronicle as literature. A century later, the text has lost its aspect of informative topicality but is still an entity with independent value. It is no longer even crucial for Jesse James to have existed in history for his character to make sense. This is one of the keys to clearing up the confusion that tends to disqualify referential literature as such, as if the real event and the system of representation were two spheres that could never come in contact.

5. Writing as Violence: Brooklyn Bridge

José Martí sought unity between science and spirit as well. He did so as a true creator, not rationalizing a system of representation, but rather allowing himself to be sincerely carried away by it. His work is a field of contradictions, of ingenious discoveries, of practically corporeal expressions of an era and a sensibility, not a series of commonplaces like that of Castelar.[8]

The dilemma was thus laid out: spirit versus matter. The Brooklyn Bridge is one of the images of the new civilization in which Martí tried to reconcile spirit and matter again and again. He wanted spirit to win over matter, and wrote: "As a poem grows in the mind of a famous bard, so grew this bridge in Roebling's mind" (XIII, 256). But deep down he knew that submission would not occur in this way: "The noise of carriages drowns out the lyre's voices. We await the new lyre, which will make chords with carriage axles" (IX, 358).

The breach between the two dimensions of reality has become clear for the *fin de siècle* man. Writing reveals the sway between inside and outside, that confrontation that wants to be harmony and therefore makes violence.[9] The first word of "Emerson" is "trembles": it refers to the writer's pen, an unworthy priest, unable to represent the spirit that "should be exalted with wings, not chipped and molded by a pen like a chisel" (XIII, 17). The first paragraph is divided into antagonisms: the unworthy, the profane, sin, molds, the commerce of the city, tumult, noise, and bustle are opposed with wings, the temple of the Universe, pure clarity, peace, a star. Between the two is the pain of writing, which attempts to reconcile, but always ends, in Martí's texts, by battling. It is not in vain—and is not only a metaphor from everyday life— that his chronicles are filled with images of war and soldiers, and of colossal violence desperate for tenderness.

He even exercises violence against Nature, when he transforms the commercial city into a colossal battleground with stone warriors with "helmets and shields of gold, and red lances" (XIII, 17). This forceful joining of what is above and what is below constitutes violence: "It feels as if I'm losing my feet and sprouting wings. It is like living by starlight, like sitting in a field of white flowers. A pale, fresh glow fills the immense, silent atmosphere" (17). This is a space where one is man and angel at once, where the spaces of heaven and earth are shared, inverting reality, so that the pale glow of the atmosphere comes not from the stars but from the flowers.

The first word in "El puente de Brooklyn" (Brooklyn Bridge) (1883) is "palpitates": from this word that refers to the heart, the very center of human life, Martí attempts to describe the construction (the making and meaning) of a stone and wire bridge. The description has several dimensions: that of the precise technological language of hydraulic cement, and that of culture. He mentions Egyptian pyramids, pelagic towers, the New Testament, Thebes and the Acropolis, Venus, a Cyclops, the Bible, the Nile, Troy, and the epic past of walled fortresses. He also incorporates Nature in such a way that the bridge is a fierce animal: a serpent, mammoth, boa, snake, octopus, monstrous body, sapper of the Universe, and spider.

Martí, desperately searching for a way to reconcile technology and existence, reached a point of contemplating the bridge in overt religiosity, as if it were an ark, or a peak, or a church that would unite all men. The verbs alone of the first four paragraphs reveal the pain in the unresolved antagonisms: palpitate, fall, feel, flow, keep up, get up, reach, clean, elevate, sustain, open, seem, precipitate, see, swarm, imagine, enter, be, dawn, seem, elevate, take, bring, highlight, bite, retain, harbor, unhinge, bunch, burn, squeeze, overturn, cut, maintain, seem, chew, tear, fall, exit, enter, hang, cross, extol, join, lower, descend, re-ascend, re-enter, cut open, support, bury, die, save. Of the fifty-three verbs that describe incessant activity, only *clean, dawn, extol, join, re-ascend,* and *save* could suggest any peace. The rest have almost adjectival force, such as *precipitate, swarm, bite, unhinge, bunch, burn, squeeze, overturn, chew, tear, cut open, bury,* and *die.*

This bridge that seems to unify is committing violence; the text describes a mammoth tooth that could have unhinged a mountain in one bite, and then refers to the cuts in the heart of a mountain. It represents the bridge as the tongue of a monstrous anteater—the multitudes have been described as ants— and there are thunderous roars and deadly rebellions of vanquished water. Giant towers barely move compared to the conglomeration of "thousands of sobbing women, screaming children, shouting policemen, forging themselves a path" (XIII, 432).

Martí wants to unify and insists on defining the bridge "as a ponderous arm of the human mind" (432), which unites past and present as well as cities:

We no longer dig deep moats around embattled fortresses. Rather cities embrace each other with arms of steel. Towns do not hold shacks for soldiers anymore, but shacks for employees, without lances or rifles, who collect coins of peace from the passing workers. Bridges are the fortresses of the modern world. Better than to open up chests is to join cities. That's what all men are now called to do: to be soldiers of the bridge! (432)

Martí fights to construct a new epic, with the modern man as protagonist, in order to reconcile oppositions. His North American contemporaries shared the same animus: they strove to unite technology and spiritual needs. John A. Roebling, for example, the engineer for the Brooklyn Bridge, worried about being the first to use the "ignoble" material, steel, and tried to humanize his construction: "The apparatus is made of stone and steel, like a hinge between two epochs; Roebling, as we have already said, was Hegelian. As Martí would say, the eternal is in the new" (Ramos, 263).

New York's newspapers from the time of the inauguration of the bridge include terms similar to Martí's. An article relegated to the second page of the *New York Daily Tribune*, called "The Brooklyn Bridge as a Text" (May 21, 1883), invokes the Roman god Terminus, the unifier, to affirm that the towers of the bridge are like temples of God, or altars. The article proclaims that the bridge is the greatest civil task ever undertaken, because it has broken insularity: "The art of man has joined together what God has put asunder, and there is no more sea."

Of course, the fact that the *New York Daily Tribune* published such reflections, with subtitles such as "The Brooklyn Bridge as Text," does not mean exactly that the North American press shared Martí's struggle to find appropriate images to describe the giant structure: this newspaper simply reproduced, in a secondary location, the Reverend John J. Chadwick's sermon from the Second Unitarian Church of Brooklyn. Although it is not insignificant that they allotted space to these words, they are nonetheless valued because they are the words of a minister. The newspaper itself informed its readers completely and coherently: it begins by giving the mythic history of bridges in general, then goes on to discuss the need to join Brooklyn and New York. There is talk about the jealousy between the two cities, the predecessors of the Roebling engineers, the construction company, the engineering problems, the details of construction, the rumors of fraud, the transport capacity, the opposition, and the preparation for the inauguration. Only then are the reverend's words presented.

The *Sun* dedicated its entire front page of May 25, 1883, to the inauguration of the bridge. Its preoccupation was the who's who of the day, that is, who was there, how the authorities and/or celebrities behaved, and how the events of the celebration were organized. The *Sun* did not exactly humanize the bridge; rather, a quotation of one of the speeches given at the inauguration compared politics to the achievement of intelligence that the suspension of the bridge represented:

Now, if our political system were guided by organized intelligence, it would not seek to repress the free play of fears, but would make provisions for their development and exercise, in accordance with the higher law of liberty and morality.

Instead of attempting to restrict suffrage, let us try to educate the voters, instead of disbanding parties, let each citizen within the party always vote, but never for a man who is unfit to hold office. Thus parties as well as voters, will be organized on the basis of intelligence.

Intelligence conquers, dominates, balances. The speakers at the inauguration shared this opinion and asserted that the bridge was "a durable monument to democracy itself." Its benefits were for everybody and its true builders were the people. Within this tranquilizing framework, the *Sun* indulges in a few lines that describe the colors of the fireworks over the night sky of both cities, united thanks to human intelligence. There is thus an elegiac contrast between the shadows, black as ink, of the New York buildings, and the golden sunset of Brooklyn. The silver, gold, pink, and deep sea-blue, separate one side from the other, suddenly united on the night of the celebration by the flames in the sky, the electric lights, the concert of illuminated windows, and red and green lights in the ports that were reflected in the white foam in the water like weightless silver.

José Martí wants that calming discourse. At the end of the second paragraph of "El puente de Brooklyn" he wrote: "Imagine seeing seated in the middle of the sky, with a radiant head for a peak, white hands, big as eagles, open in a sign of peace over the earth, Liberty, which has given this city such a daughter. Liberty is the mother of the new world that is dawning. And it seems as if a sun is rising over these two towers" (XIII, 423). Reading this paragraph today is as tranquilizing as the North American descriptions that compare the bridge to progress and democracy. After all, it does not seem incongruous that he should allude to the Statue of Liberty. But if one verifies a few dates, Martí's image begins to create some discomfort. "El puente de Brooklyn" was published in 1883, and the statue not only does not have open hands, but it also did not arrive in New York until 1887. One could infer that comparing this city with liberty was in the spirit of the times, which is why the French donated the Statue of Liberty to New York. But the "vision" is only the first of a series of fairly suprareal or hyperreal visions that gradually invade the text.

On the one hand, Martí uses the discourse of technology, which is quantification (Ramos, 263).[10] The amount of numbers, weights, details, and measurements that he gives in "El puente de Brooklyn" is notable and conscientious, but something has occurred on the inside of this referential language. J. Starobinski says the following about the language of quantification: "La géométrie est le langage de la raison dans l'univers des signes. Elle reprend toutes les formes en leur commencement—à leurs principaux niveaux d'un système de points de lignes, et de proportions constantes. Tout surcroît, toute irrégularité apparait des lors comme l'intrusion du mal."[11]

The "intrusion of evil," seen thus, is constant in Martí's texts. Because if the sense of quantification is that it reduces and homogenizes, Martí expresses himself through unique images created by each subject, through exception, deviation from all norms, heterogeneity, and subjectivity. There is, then, a clash of discourses that cannot help being violent and ends, at the very least, in expressionist hallucinations. It is obvious that conventional language could be of no use to this sensibility, since there is nothing tranquilizing in those magic cables or light tubes of an invasive and monstrous bridge.

Admiration for the achievements of technology and awareness of the benefits of communication and labor do not translate into the required symmetry or harmony. Hallucinations tend to be preceded by the verb "to seem." He talks about unborn soldiers, blocks of granite, and the bridge as if it were a man who united the lives of others. He thus changes the point of view: he speaks from the crowd—"the mob that was pushing us along"—and later as if he were observing from the sky—"at our feet sits the bridge." He speaks from the immediate present, then repositions himself to view the same scene as if from the classical past, from the perspective of the Bible, of Thebes, and the Acropolis. His strange descriptions of the bridge continue, "it had spans for antlers."

When the *Sun* attempted a description of the bridge as if seen from above on May 25, 1883, it gave the rational explanation of what a reporter would see if he went up in a balloon:

From a balloon, if a reporter could have inhabited the tiny one that was floating in the sky over the structure, the general picture would have shown, not the graceful outlines of the massive span with its live roadways, but the river beneath, with trails of foam following the turtle-like ferryboats, and the beetle-like tugboats, and the rippling wake of the mosquito-like small craft that moved beneath. The East River seemed to be for the time an aqueous Broadway. The president ran his eye around the horizon with the air of one appreciating the happy combination of the works of God and man. He filled his insides from the refreshing breeze . . . calculating the fishing advantages afforded by the $15,000,000 highway.

The animalization of the boats and steamboats in this text coincides with Martí's description of "speaking messengers and white ants that bump into each other on the river, cross their antennae, deliver their message and then part" (XIII, 341). But the similarities end there; Martí would not have incorporated the balloon into his text. Worse still is the breach opened by the quantifying commentary of the *Sun* about the satisfaction and calculation of the president.

6. Emerson: The Unquantifiable

José Martí may have accepted the hierarchy that North American newspapers applied to the topics that he covered, but he did not say the same things about those topics. As a writer and mediator, he tells a different story about the same episode. To Martí, for example, Emerson was not the man who achieved public success, but the one who pursued his work despite the interference of mediocre people, removing himself from the noisy life of commerce. Martí was not so much interested in the philosopher's contribution to religious thinking as he was in his approach to roots, to Nature, and his work with writing. He pays no attention to the cause of death or to any chronology, because Martí believed in a continuous flow of time that dissolves into the unity of the great chain of existence.

The *New York Times* dedicated more than five columns in its first two pages to represent Ralph Waldo Emerson's last moments, the story of his life, his ascending achievements and notable encounters, his influences on others, and noteworthy phrases from and commentary on his work. But his greatest quality, according to the *Times*, was that there was no greater preoccupation on the planet or mystical immersion for Emerson that would make him forget his family duties. This thinker was an example to enrich "in some sort our national life, for living as high as we think is rarer than the rarest genius." The conclusion is striking because the *New York Times* analyzes Emerson's work exhaustively, and even understands its importance in the construction of the new continent. Its text could almost coincide, point by point, with Martí's, except for the burial of history:

Our age is retrospective. It builds the sepulchers of our fathers. It writes biographies, histories and criticism. The foregoing generations beheld God and Nature face to face: we do so through their eyes. Why should we not also enjoy an original relation to the universe? Why should we not have a poetry and philosophy of insight, and not of tradition, and a religion by revelation to us, and not the history of theirs . . . The sun shines today, also. There is more wood and flax in the fields. There are new lands, new men, new thoughts. Let us demand our own works and laws and worship.[12]

Now this priest, this patriarch who knew how to live because he knew how to break away, who never "rented his mind, or his language, or his conscience" (XIII, 25)—this "Emerson" of Martí's—has little to do with the institutionalized and recognized "Mr. Emerson" that the *Times* presents. It is more than just a question of nuances and point of view. The paragraph quoted from the *Times* is preceded and followed by a defense of Emerson's wisdom for not publishing trivialities: "Had all writers followed his example how immeasurably libraries would have been reduced," notes the article approvingly, adding that "Emerson is a pattern to all mere book-makers present and to come. If he had done nothing else than to inculcate by example the economy of print, he would deserve a separate niche in the temple of literary fame."

For Martí, he was a giant in search of the secret of the universe, which he found in the "borders of the Gold eagle" (XIII, 27). He traveled in leaps and did not compromise for those who could not follow the rhythm of his writing. It is precisely in this similarity that Martí affirms the unquantifiable, that which can never be commandeered by industrialism: art is nature created by man; nature is at man's service, not so that he can transform it and benefit from its material resources, but so that he can learn from its moral order and perfect his judgment (25).

But according to Martí, the order of reality was in crisis in *fin de siècle* sensibilities. Thus he wrote: "It is like having one's skull populated with stars, an interior vault, silent and vast, that illuminated the peaceful night and made it sacred! Magnificent world" (XIII, 20). He does not distinguish between the interior and exterior worlds. Liberty, for him, is to be outside the control of institutions. He says as much in "Emerson": "There was never a man more free from the pressures of men and of his time . . . He obeyed no system, which seemed to him a blind and serf-like act; he created no system, which seemed to him the act of a thin, low, and envious mind" (XIII, 20).

7. Brooklyn: The Explosion and Condensation of Opposites

José Martí, the chronicler, tried to reconcile the journalistic language of reason, of homogenizing geometry, with his own searching and inquisitive discourse. To understand the stone and steel behemoth that is erected before him, and to justify describing it with marrow and nerves, he says in "El puente de Brooklyn" that it is law "that any organism invented by man, that dominates or fertilizes the earth, is bound to bear a resemblance to man" (IX, 428). The problem is that, even though it is man's invention, the bridge is not an organism.

Thus the extreme hallucinatory level comes when Martí describes the way in which the bases for the bridge were built: the *Caisson*, or box of pine boards, was made with "screws as thick as trees, twisted and gigantic, as a lunatic's ideas must appear in his illuminated brain" (IX, 428). The construction of the *Caisson* also captivated the North American press of the time, but for Martí it represented such violence against Nature that he describes it as initiating a journey toward hell. He talks about struggles, roars, lights that cannot be turned off, an iron well like Limbo, where "men pass, grave and silent through the entrance, and cold, anxious, white, and lugubrious as ghosts at the exit, *through a sort of antechamber*, or a bolt of air, *with two doors, one to the upper well, and another to the cave, which are never open at the same time*" (429; italics mine).

There is also talk of a fierce army, with concave jaws and open gullets, of a dredge that swallows, of powerful jawbones, mud, sand, pieces of rock, the noise of chains, and a strange factory. Many workers did in fact die working on the *Caisson*, that box "with human bowels" (IX, 430). Here Martí reaches the paroxysm of hallucination: "And the construction workers fit in at that height, like the wooden toys of children in the tower of Crandall's game. There were stones whose slightest touch would, like a human finger upon a butterfly's wing, destroy the workers' bodies or uncover their skulls. Oh, unknown workers, oh beautiful martyrs, entrails of greatness, cement of the eternal concrete, *worms of glory!*" (430).

The symbol has also reached its apex. Martí has so carefully chosen his words that the reference to an innocent childhood game is as chilling as the uncovered skulls and destroyed bodies. Because Prudence Crandall—according to *Encyclopaedia Britannica*—was a schoolteacher arrested in Connecticut in 1833 for having accepted a black student; she was condemned to five years of public ostracism.

8. Modes of Constructing the Subject: Toward Dis-identification

Returning to the axis of colonizing/colonized writing, it is worth noting that the observing gaze exercises power over what is observed (the object), as it imposes the rules of its ideological game. Nevertheless, when the subject of the gaze is "peripheral," what is revealed is not only the object of the gaze, but the rules of the game itself. In fact, Martí is the exile who looks and comments upon the structure of power that has rejected and threatened to silence him. In the act of observing/writing, he recreates (and alters, as we have seen) not only the system of representation but also the means of appropriating elements of the dominant culture from a different location and impregnating them with alternate, independent meanings.

Michel Pêcheux explains three different modes of construction of the subject confronted with colonial power (or neocolonial, we should say, with respect to

Martí and the United States).[13] The first is identification with power. The second is "counter-identification" (reproduction of the negative aspect of the relation, emphasis on the act of distancing). The third is "dis-identification," or the product of political and discursive practices that work within and counter to the dominant ideology. This third modality recognizes the inescapable existence of the dominant ideology, but believes in the possibility of transformation. Thus, dis-identification is a working of the subject, not just its abolition (169). According to Pêcheux, linguistic meaning has a material weight because it is a signifier within the cultural battle (111).

One superlative example of this change in meaning is the one already cited from "Coney Island," in which prosperity is tantamount to spiritual vacuousness. Another example can be found in "El puente de Brooklyn" (1883), in which Martí transfers the semantic axis, by means of oxymoron, turning the "unknown workers" that built the bridge into "worms of glory" (155). Words no longer hold their traditional meanings: eagles do not signify birds of prey in "El puente de Brooklyn" or in "Emerson" (1882), and in "El poeta Walt Whitman" (1892), the entozoa, a gastro-intestinal parasite, is sanctified (XIII, 134). The displacements are multiple, but they serve to describe the North American social scene to its readers: the cities are ovens, islands are baskets, and steam engines are ants that communicate by crossing their antennae (IX, 431). The Ohio River is a herd of colts that *speeds* along with winged helmets, and the entire earth spins with the dice on New York game tables (IX, 353). An antislavery speech is turned into vengeful images that come out of the portraits on the wall and into a rain of burning stones (XIII, 64). Urban crowds are barbaric armies, stone warriors with golden shields and helmets and red lances (XIII, 17).

The construction of the subject changes throughout Martí's chronicles, since his own experience in New York changed over the years. His exile in North America can be divided into three distinct phases. I have already cited several texts from the first stage, 1881–1884; Martí's masterpieces from this time communicate the pangs of exile, his culture shock and the enigmas of time and space, the search for harmonies and the reconciliation of opposites, as in his portrait of Emerson and his account of the inauguration of the Brooklyn Bridge. The second stage, 1884–1892, is marked by Martí's critical radicalization and his gradual break from the qualities we generally associate with exilic writing today: homesickness, nostalgia, marginalization. This period begins with his protests of the inequitable trade agreement signed between Mexico and the United States; and its definitive moment comes in 1886, when Martí recognizes the possibility that North American expansionists will eventually target Cuba. This is the year in which Martí establishes ties with Cuban tobacco workers in Florida, the year of his discouragement with labor strikes and the death sentences of the Chicago anarchists. His radicalization advances, and in 1889 Martí writes about North American rapacity in such pieces as "El Congreso de Washington" (The Washington Congress), "Madre América" (Mother America), and *La Edad de Oro* (The Golden Age). The year 1891 sees the International Monetary Conference and the writing of *Nuestra América* (Our America). Further radicalization marks the change that begins the third and final phase of Martí's exile. This last stage is outside the scope of our study of Martí's *Escenas norteamericanas*, since at that time he renounces his affiliation with Spanish American newspapers. In 1892 Martí founds the Cuban Revolutionary Party, and in April 1895 makes his final return to Cuba.

In the second phase, the text about General Grant (1885) marks a difference in tone from those that came before, while still trying to maintain equilibrium: "He may have been guilty; but his crime will always be lesser than his greatness" (XIII, 43). In his marvelous chronicle about the Charleston earthquake, the perfect order of the beginning—of the white houses and the prosperity propelled by the triumph of whites over blacks—will be destroyed by unbridled Nature. Unlike the *Sun*, the *New York Times*, the *Baltimore Sun*, or the *Tribune* (September, 1886), Martí is not interested in material damage. What intrigues him is the explosion that rises from deep within the earth to upset the well-trimmed hedges of civilization (XIII, 68). He establishes in the writing a relationship with nature that can exist only on the page, as it does violence to the realist, *costumbrista*, romantic, and even liberal systems of representation. The *Sun* (September 2, 3, and 4, 1886), like Martí's text, describes the people who came running naked and shouting into the street, the undulation of the train whose cars rose and fell as it galloped along, the snake-like rails and clocks that stopped when the quake began, and the terrible noise of the upheaval. The text mentions two people who jumped off their balconies in fright, religious orgies of the blacks, and the possible scientific reasons for the quake. But whereas the *Sun* mentions *a* fallen statue, Martí amplifies this to "the statues have descended from their pedestals" (70). The *Sun's* information about the many births that occurred after the first tremor on September 4 turns into the image of two laughing twins being born in a blue tent at the same time as the earthquake.

9. Chaos and Harmony

José Martí resorts to Nature to shake the system of representation. Reason and intelligence were the instruments that romantics, *costumbristas*, realists, positivists, and even the liberal journalists who were Martí's contemporaries used to tame the barbarism of nature. Industry imposed itself on hidden disorder, homogenizing and ordering. But for Martí, Nature would return to its proper course, a reality that he felt had become disordered, heterogeneous, and in a state of crisis. The best chronicles that he wrote about North American writers (Emerson, Whitman, Longfellow), all posit Nature as the governing force that destroys the molds imposed by civilization and achieves a degree of harmony. In his text about the Charleston earthquake it is Nature—in this case the catastrophe—that literally unearths the roots of human existence and the truth about each man.

The *New York Times*, the *Baltimore Sun*, and the *Tribune* report the catastrophe by accumulating facts and names in a succession of wires that begin with the date and location of the event. Each wire is like a chapter of a whole, but is also absolutely independent. They give statistics about material losses, the number of persons known to be wounded, and the names of the dead; they print testimonies as well as *mises en scène* of the earthquake.

Past and present alternate in the paragraphs of "El terremoto de Charleston" and sentences are longer or shorter according to the rhythm they are trying to achieve. Although every detail comes from a newspaper, the mimeticism of the representation is interrupted by extraordinary images. The letter "r" abounds, sentences are cut off, and the rhythm seems to reverberate like a locomotive. "To say it is to see it" (XIII, 67), Martí wrote, immediately following with expressions such as "the sound swelled up" and "men flapped about like half-winged birds."[14] Every detail comes from a newspaper, but certainly no other text included the flapping men, nor such questions as: "Who grabbed the city by the waist, shaking it in the air, with a terrible and twisted hand?" (67).

The indistinct sound is heard again: people spin around as if studying the best exit. They flee in every direction: the wave below grows and undulates; each person believes there is a tiger upon him.

Some fall to their knees: others throw themselves flat on the ground: rich old people are carried in the arms of their faithful servants: cracks open in the earth: walls wave like cloth in the wind and cornices knock together high atop the buildings: the beasts' horror increases that of the people: horses unable to break free of their carriages overturn them with the jerking of their flanks: one folds his forelegs: others sniff the ground: another's eyes shine red in the firelight, his body trembles like sugarcane in a storm: what frightful drum raises this battle from the entrails of the earth? (68)

Tenses, syntax, and punctuation are dislocated. Spanish phonetics create meaning; the text reports a factual event while reflecting on its own writing, at times as explicitly as when Martí analyzes the rhythm of the blacks' prayers. The narrator seems to withdraw to another order having nothing to do with the events in Charleston, a state that can perhaps be called the equilibrium of creation.

A different logic deconstructs the representation; the "arrogant whites" join "their voices humbly" to the hymns of the blacks (XIII, 70). Martí has begun to trace different types of alliances in the heart of society. He realizes, as can be seen in "Terremoto de Charleston," that the time has come for this continent that declared itself racially mixed, syncretic, a melting pot, to flow with its own voice, a voice which should grow and change naturally as it appropriates from all of its cultures and all of its pasts. This voice of the continent is legitimized—like racial mixing—when its various languages pass through the filter of experience, of their own history, and of nature. Martí retains a moving, visionary tone: "with that whole universe of wings beating inside his head, man is nothing more than one of those shining bubbles that dance blindly in a ray of sunshine! Poor warrior of the air, covered with gold, always slammed to earth by an enemy he can't see, always getting up confused from the blow, rushing off to a new battle" (66).[15]

Martí may have been able to "literaturize" the information taken from newspapers, but the axis that structures "Terremoto de Charleston" is nowhere to be found in the local dailies; only for Martí does the catastrophe equalize social classes and races. North American newspapers discuss the people who flee their houses and the blacks who fall into religious deliriums, but in Martí's chronicle terrified whites join in the primitive African rituals, the earthquake having unleashed ancient needs that stimulate behaviors and even relationships contrary to the norm.

This difference in interpretation cannot be attributed to Martí's Spanish-American origin as opposed to the yankee rationalism of the New York journalists. Another text published on May 26, 1881, in *La Opinión Nacional* from Caracas by the Venezuelan writer Arístedes Rojas, reconstructs the mythical story of another earthquake that took place in Caracas on March 26, 1812. In this chronicle, Nature is allied with the Church: both are depicted as barbarous, enemies of Progress and Reason. What is valorized in this text is human will, especially the will of the Liberator, Simón Bolívar, who managed to overcome Nature and defeat fanaticism. Geography therefore is insufficient to explain the dislocation of language and representation in Martí's writing.

10. The Anarchists

In the same year, 1886, the first note that Martí wrote about the Chicago anarchists condemns them. This is striking because he represents the anarchists as a version of the Others that disrupt the established order with their irrational backwardness: the text emphasizes the foreignness of these people who do not understand the mechanics of democracy. The anarchists come from a European "there": "Three of them did not even understand the language in which they were being condemned," wrote Martí, with the scorn of one exile toward another who has not known how to confront the codes of the nation (*Crónicas*,

212). These recent arivals do not understand the "here," which is why "They suggested the barbarous remedies imagined in those countries where the downtrodden have neither speech nor vote," unlike here "where the most wretched is free to express the words in his mouth . . . and can cast with his hand the vote that enacts the laws" (212). It is not the case that Martí idealized the "here" represented by the United States, since in the same text that nation is described in terms of egoism and the agony of the poor. But he is appalled by the violence and disdain or incomprehension of a system that for Martí, considering his experience in colonial Cuba and the collective experience of his desired Spanish American family of nations, represents admirable values: the electoral process and legal liberty that exist in the United States.

Martí returns to the subject of the anarchists a few months after his dazzling ode to Walt Whitman. But now his point of view has changed entirely: although clearly European, the anarchist is no longer an outsider to be ostracized even through language; instead he is the victim of a social system that is unjust and cruel to the poor. Martí never endorses terrorism, but now he clearly aligns himself with the working masses and sees the system itself as the Other. In 1888 he sympathizes with "the exhausted masses that suffer greater pains each day" (*Crónicas*, 227). His voice is no longer that of a dazzled transient, but rather is marked by solid and critical identification with social struggle. Thus he states that "to measure the full depths of human desperation . . . it is necessary to live exiled from one's homeland or from humanity" (229).

Empathy can be read here as the mark of exile. There is a slow process of identification with certain areas of the abject. As Judith Butler explains, the abject designates the "uninhabitable" areas of social life, which are, nonetheless, populated by those who do not enjoy the status of subjects.[16] Inclusion/exclusion and displacement of inside and outside are other ways to approach this writing, which inverts the terms of colonial discourse.

11. In Search of a Shared Identity

In order to construct himself as a subject, Martí had to articulate the Other (the United States) as different from the Us (Spanish America) by means of repetitions and displacements of meaning. He faced the double difficulty of presenting himself, the chronicler, before the metropolis, but also before the periphery that was his own world of reference, his receiving public. Martí had to find his own discourse in the face of the hyperactive "seven-league-giant" (his well-known depiction of the U.S.). However, despite his desire to insert the domain of the "Us" into his texts, that represented "Us" had divergent interests in reality. As a matter of fact, the nature of culture casts doubt upon vernacular definitions of community. Seen in this way, identity appears not only as a collective fiction, but also as an arena for negotiation and conflict. National identity and Spanish America's relationship with the United States were flagrantly disputed during the time that Martí wrote his chronicles, as is suggested in the conflicts that sometimes arose between him and his editors. The North America Martí depicted—despite his personal admiration of progress and the notion of liberty—was not always in keeping with the image that liberal men of letters preferred to present.

His transforming gaze—to follow the definition of the three stages of construction of the subject—was not, then, always shared by other Spanish American men of letters who were more anxious to live the identification with the United States as a model for their countries' development than to distance themselves from that nation with criticism. Thus, less than a year after Martí began his collaboration with the Caracas newspaper *La Opinión Nacional,* its editor, Fausto Teodoro Aldrey, asked him for more news and less literature. What's more, he requested that Martí alter his political judgments about the United States (Quesada, 97–99): Martí refused and eventually resigned from the paper, as mentioned before. A similar situation developed with the Buenos Aires paper *La Nación*, when Bartolomé Mitre supressed entire paragraphs of Martí's work. Even Sarmiento, despite his admiration of Martí as a writer, demanded that as *La Nación*'s New York correspondent he be "our eye that observes human movement where it is most accelerated, most intellectual, most free . . . in order to show us the right road." He adds: "I would like Martí to give us a little less Martí, a little less of the Latin, less of the Spanish race and less South America, for a little more yankee" (Quesada, 113). This time José Martí persists, however, and manages to keep publishing his chronicles in *La Nación* without betraying himself, thus inserting them into the Spanish American discursive field.

12. Truth Is Only a Consensus

Martí is always there observing, trying to reproduce the palpitations of the United States for his Spanish American readers. He resorts again and again to the narrative strategy of the immediate witness. In "El centenario americano" (1889), although Martí admits that only "known ladies" and "men of profit" were admitted to the celebrations, his descriptions contain the minute detail of a guest sitting in the front row. He comments on flowers in a buttonhole, a pendant around a neck, the brocade of a skirt, avidity in front of the food table, a young girl dressed in white who blows kisses from afar, and a man with his felt hat on backward. His authority is that of first-hand knowledge, of one who has been there. It does not matter that it is perfectly obvious that this is only a strategy. The same approach is repeated in "Terremoto de Charleston" (1886) and in "Como se crea un pueblo nuevo en los Estados Unidos (How a new town is created in the United States) (1889), despite the impossibility of his having been present at the earthquake, or among the settlers advancing to take over land in Oklahoma.

It is curious that Martí's practice of narrating directly events he could not possibly have witnessed did not offend his readers' sensibilities or lessen his credibility. What cost him credibility was more often the content of the chronicles itself, in other words *what* was told and not *how* it was told. Martí caused dismay by presenting an image of the United States that was not the one the editors wanted to read, one that did not accord with their prior assumptions. Truth is nothing more than consensus. The difference between the position of the producer and that of his readers (their not only geographic but ideological locations as well) reveals itself in "Narraciones fantásticas" (Fantastic narrations). The text begins with a summer celebration, then goes on at length about:

ball players who have left the University in order to play ball for a living, because as lawyers or doctors the money would be too little and it would be a lot more work. Whereas for their skill in catching a long ball . . . or zipping around the four sides of the diamond that they play on, they not only gain fame in their countries . . . as well as cheers from ladies well versed in the game, but enormous salaries too, so big that some of these ball players receive more for two months' work than a bank director, or University dean, or secretary of a department in Washington. (*Crónicas*, 256)

Amazement is not the tenor of the rest of the chronicle, which is mostly dedicated to describing the 1888 selection of presidential candidates for the Republican and Democratic parties. Martí undeniably dramatizes the enthusiasm that Cleveland's election produced among those present (261–62), but today's reader would likely find the description of baseball compelling, and that of the election almost boring. This was not the effect on the reader of the time, as can be seen in the changes made to "Narraciones fantásticas" (see chapter 3).

13. Between Transparency and Difference

Changing the location of the gaze, as occurs in *Escenas norteamericanas*, also changes the terms of the powerful/powerless, center/periphery, and Us/Them relationships. If a sketch of customs is found in Martí's writing, then we can no longer speak of normalization: the sketch does not aim to universalize, since the subject narrates from his own present, involving the witness who observes (from a slight distance) as from a tower of love and fear. In terms of domesticability and the work force, the mirror is inverted. The Cuban exile's gaze measures the positive and negative changes that are being imposed on Spanish America, calculating in reverse: he sees, yes, and even admires the productive capacity of his Other, but he keeps his distance. He does not project or identify himself: he, the savage, the colonized, observes the project of "civilization" that is being imposed and warns against the empty materialism it entails.

In terms of the landscape and the homogenized "they," Martí does the opposite of what a subject in a position of power would do in order to defend his location or gaze: Lefebvre refers to the strategy of representation of the powerful as the "illusion of transparency." Transparent space assumes that the world is a space of mimetic representation that tends toward homogeneity and the negation of difference.[17]

Mimesis is an imperial form of representing reality. At the same time, it had a very specific political/aesthetic weight at the time that the *Escenas norteamericanas* were written. Not only was the European discussion about Zola taking place, but the New York intellectual field was divided between idealists and realists, as is reflected in Martí's chronicles. As a proponent of subjectivism, his tendency was, for example, to praise Edmund Clarence Stedman, an idealist literary critic, and to reject William Dean Howells, a spokesman for realism and the incipient socialism. Martí considered Howells to be false and coarse, since "to reproduce is not to create" (XI, 360–61). The problem is that Stedman sheltered himself in the indifference of aestheticism, while Howells took on social causes similar to those of Martí, such as criticizing the execution of the Chicago anarchists. Martí, writing from "the bowels of the monster," wants neither evasion nor mimesis nor false transparency. For Martí, writing should be a tool for human improvement, a space of condensation in which to reconcile the transcendent and material aspects of social existence.

There is not, then, a truth that can pretend to be homogenous and universalizing. There is always interruption, always a "but."

In "El centenario americano" (The American centennial) (1889), Martí makes the elitist parade a stylistic device: each person becomes his or her attribute, be it a uniform, clothing, or the "brand" of an illustrious family name. In the midst of all the pomp, Martí introduces lines that disrupt the order: there is "an inebriated girl covered with diamonds," the police are forced to remove the president from the dance by clubbing him, a misshapen buffoon tells funny stories, and there are men in the dressing rooms "falling on their faces" from too much drink (*Crónicas*, 300). Martí's values are evident in this assemblage: the military uniform is hideous, except when it defends against tyranny (303), and patriotic glory does not reside "in stocks, bonds, or sumptuous houses" but in heroes, in the flag, and in patriotic sentiment (396).

The gaze is always heterogeneous and the representation carefully balanced. "Como se crea un pueblo nuevo en los Estados Unidos" (How a new town is created in the United States) (1889), begins by telling what "El centenario

Americano" leaves out: vote grubbers, electoral corruption, the ugliness of railroads that fill New York with "smoke and fright," the crowding of flags and up-ended beams for the celebration, and the dark crowd that gathers to see the remains of the terrible Central Railway warehouse fire: "ill-smelling lads with tobacco-stained lips, young laboring women dressed in filthy silk and velvet, barefoot boys with their fathers' overcoats, black-nosed vagabonds . . ." (*Crónicas*, 281).

The gesture of relocation in the *Escenas norteamericanas* is complex. It begins with the difficulty of constructing a location from the margin. Then it must also construct a discourse that can be understood by Spanish America, which it in turn modifies as his place of belonging. José Martí is not only renewing aesthetics, together with other modernist writers; he also wants to change the ways of thinking reality. He writes from the margins of the gaze—not with the attitude of inferiority expected of the subject confronted by Empire, but with a transforming will. He does not seek to subject or be subjected, but to *create*. In "Darwin y el Talmud" he writes: "The human journey consists of reaching the country that is described within us" (XV, 403). His gaze is filled with willfulness, with a different form of power, as if he were reproducing again and again Fouillé's paraphrase of Boileau quoted previously: "I do not think about things to come simply because they will be; rather, those things will be in part because I think them."[18] Thus Martí's oeuvre, including the chronicles that refer to North America, is a perpetual reflection on being, or having the duty of being, Spanish American.

If Martí's system of representation seems to displace reality outside or beyond his texts, his technique in fact managed to reach and capture that reality while it was still alive. Martí achieved this with a transfiguring language, open to artifice, and capable of converting that same reality into the source of an autonomous literary discourse.

Martí developed his oeuvre in a time of dispersion and drastic scientific, political, cultural, and economic shifts. At the turn of the century, the Spanish America of the independence centennials no longer resembled the village-based America of the civil wars and the national post-independence organizations. Martí was the first to capture the modernity that had seemed so inexpressible. He was also one of the first to understand—along with Manuel Gutiérrez Nájera—that that perception did not belong in books alone. This fleeting and constantly developing reality could only be captured with a language that shared the same rhythm, the same fleeting nature, mutability, and immediacy. At the same time, this language had to express the potency of these changes with an equally inventive poetics that was tense and continually dissatisfied with itself. This language found its new epic in the journalistic chronicle and turned it, like the ancient sagas, into a space of battle and creation, strewn with victories and defeats.

Chapter 6

Conclusion
Adventure and Transgression in Writing and Reading

This is not the place to summarize the relationship of the *Escenas norteamericanas* to the press of the United States or of Spanish America, or the influences Martí's texts underwent and in turn exerted on the literature of the time. Nor is this the place to rethink the topic of the exilic gaze in Martí's writing. What is appropriate here is simply to insist on the need to rediscover the modernist chronicles in order that justice may be done to a vast literary production that transformed Spanish American prose and the entire culture of the *fin de siècle*. Even the fact of such a transformation remains controversial and has been insufficiently discussed.

Rediscovering the chronicles is no less than an act of transgression, because it is a transgression and an adventure to accept that a new literature can spring from journalism, to ask what a genre is or, even worse, what literature is and why one text is "art" and another is not. The chronicle is a hybrid, marginal and excluded, rarely taken seriously by the institutions of literature or journalism, since it is not definitively one or the other. The elements that liken it to each one have served only to prompt the other to ignore, dismiss, or disdain it.

It is curious that the chronicle emerged at a time when the specialization of functions and discourses was just beginning. Politicians claimed the state discourse, literature established its autonomy within the aesthetic sphere, and journalism was defining its space. Journalism is meant to be the objective witness of significant current events. This implies a pact with the reader that, although what is told may seem incredible, it is completely factual. In literature, on the contrary, what is told may or may not *seem* real, but no claim is made that it ever occurred outside the author's imagination.

The chronicle tends to focus on the details of daily life and on narration. It indulges in originalities that break the rules of journalism, such as the irruption of subjectivism. Chronicles do not respect chronological order, credibility, the narrative structure of news stories, or the duty to answer the six basic questions—who, what, when, where, how, and why.

The chronicle does not invent the events it relates, but it differs from journalism in the way it reproduces reality. The texts Martí wrote as a correspondent in

New York do not adhere to the conventions of mimetic representation, but his subjectivism does not betray reality. On the contrary, subjectivism allows Martí to approach reality in another way, in order to rediscover its essence; subjectivism allows Martí to overcome his era's exhausted confidence in the appearance of things.

Martí describes events through mechanisms such as analogy, symbolism, impressionism, expressionism, and musicality. He produces abundant images that are constructions of his own thought and do not exist outside the space of the text. The result is a chronicle that does not remove the reader from the dimension of the reality of events or lose its referential balance, but nonetheless introduces a mode of perception that mythologizes or transcendentalizes reality.

Rereading the modernist chronicles, as we have done, contributes to the study of this literary period, especially if it manages to reveal José Martí's role as the founder of a new way of writing. But another objective of this study has been to question the conventions of reading itself for what they reveal about the relations between art and society. By considering the chronicle as an inflection point between journalism and literature, we discover that our way of interpreting or constructing the autonomy of discourses has deformed our consideration of the "literary" in particular. Facts have been left to other disciplines, as if what is aesthetic and literary could allude only to emotion or imagination, as if the "literariness" of a text diminished with an increase in referentiality. Other written discourses then seem exempt from the qualities that inform literature, as if they were not also developed representations, configurations of the world, rationalizations and elaborations, which find a certain form according to their era. The real referent has been confused with the system of representation, as if the objective parts of a text were "the truth" and not a narrative strategy.

This dissociation between the world of real events and that of artistic creation cannot be disregarded as a source of the accusations of elitism and aestheticism against modernist writers. As we have seen, it is one thing to analyze the realization of the poetic act as a definition of the separate domain of literary discourse and another to believe that this realization is aestheticizing in the pejorative sense that it deforms reality, ignores events, and only beautifies the status quo. The poetic act instead permits the formation of codes that in turn generate the capacity to perceive reality in a new way.

This new way of understanding writing is already very clear in Martí's chronicles. It does not matter that in this case the texts were also produced with a moralizing intention; that intention is of another order. Martí's words have two meanings: the transparent and centrifugal meaning that pertains to journalism, as well as the poetic meaning assigned by the writing itself and the words' relationship to each other.

Literary autonomy represented a break with the traditional writing system. This, of course, is true not only in Spanish America. But the chronicle itself is an even stronger break, because from the start it both questions and participates in that autonomy. It contradicts and reinforces it, bringing in criteria that writing systems have just begun to explain a century later. Modernist prose and poetry were the first to understand and develop this change in this hemisphere.

Martí's chronicles not only participate in the revolution of word handling, they also show how stereotypical the understanding of poetic language was and still is. To this day poetry is characterized by its potential for removing words from their usual meanings in order to reveal multiple meanings, according to the writer's technical ability. No two things are more opposed, in theory, than a poem and a journalistic chronicle. Martí's chronicles were produced under all the conditions that supposedly corrupt journalistic texts, including the need to choose current and topical subjects, and to write extremely quickly. The chronicles cannot be called "disinterested" texts, since Martí earned a living as a journalist. Worst of all, they were written for a specific, massive readership with certain demands and expectations. Despite all of this, it is here, in Martí's chronicles, that we find what today qualifies as poetic language.

These categories of the literary surround a power distribution mechanism. Artistic creation remains outside of the productive, useful world, and acquires the value of intellectual or spiritual pleasure. The image of the world is ordered from different areas of written discourse: these include history, academia, journalism, and science. But the rigidity of these categories hides the reality of writing: all texts respond to a process of selection, or an ordering principle. This does not mean that any written discourse is literature, since the latter is constructed on the artistic use of language as a primary value; but it does mean that the predominant definition of journalism prevents people from realizing that everything they read is questionable, that writing is not "reality" but rather representation.

The poeticization of the real is part of what a modernist chronicle is. The new poetics produced a new literary genre. This means a new method of conceptualizing reality, of internal and external composition and orientation, which in this case forms its own space by oscillating between the literary and journalistic discourses.

The modernist chronicle includes some additional elements. It selects current themes, and tends toward the fragmentary, toward visions of multiplicity, but without losing the comprehensiveness and coherence that are attractive to the reader. The chronicle includes a stylization of the literary subject, description through images that express an idea, and a wide range of stylistic devices. Referential and self-referential styles appear, with frequent reflections on literature itself, on the city as setting, and on culture as a natural attribute.

For a text to be literary, it must have an index of originality, the opposite of the cliché: its value is its *way* of saying something. Rubén Darío, perhaps the modernist most accused of elitism, expressed this idea clearly: clichés in expression accompany mental clichés. This is why modernism was so significant for the literary and social transformation of the *fin de siècle*: although modernists' poetry reached only a limited audience, their journalism enjoyed a vast sphere of influence.

As an art form, literature cannot be seen as a category separate from the social process that contains it: it is an act of historical solidarity and participates in the multiplicity of cultural practice, as Barthes and Williams claimed. This makes the rereading of José Martí's chronicles so fascinating. Their "impurity" within the divisions of discourses—that is, their marginality with respect to established categories—constitutes what Martí aspired to in his writing: they break away from clichés and allow for new forms of perception. By insisting on originality and nonrepetition, the chronicles find the way of real rupture: to confront with one's own experience what is learned is to question it, revise it, and leave it only what it has proven meaningful or transformed into another form of truth.

Martí's chronicles are a product of this process. They include many systems of representation, and the result of confrontation and personal mixture constitutes his novelty and originality. The aesthetic he proposes is not an imitation of anything: it surpasses the molds of what came before, thus founding in Spanish America a new way of relating the elements of language and reality.

Originality, for Martí, was equivalent to authenticity; that is why he insisted so much that each period has its own language, as does each creator. And it is true, as many have said, that modernist poetics gave Spanish American literature its own voice for the first time. But what is interesting is the force this unique voice projects through the chronicles. Perhaps its value is to be found, even more than in its break with tradition, in its foundation of a new way of writing. Seen thus, the chronicle's hybrid nature is not a detraction, but rather the most appropriate expression of a new poetic conception. In the prologue to "Poema del Niágara" Martí concludes that the place for ideas is in journalism: it is the space of the impermanent, of communication, and of majority readership. It is the only space that allows the entrance of life, which is precisely the only legitimate issue in *fin de siècle* literature.

In a time of epistemological ruptures, when discursive heterogeneity was a destabilizing tension, Martí created a space of condensation and struggle. In the chronicle idealism is based in reality. History and immediacy gravitate toward the subjective, ordering "I" in an attempt to rebuild some kind of harmony. A space of condensation is a dialectic encounter that is neither resolved nor static, and the chronicle epitomizes that space because it contains all mixtures converted into a single unity, which is autonomous and as contradictory as its time.

The chronicle proposes a new epic, with modern man as protagonist. It is narrated through an "I" that seeks to incorporate the universe into himself, a collective "I" that strives to express life in its entirety. It is based on a new system of representation able to relate different forms of existence, a system based upon exploring and assimilating to the maximum the resources known to enrich writing technique. Every idea is expressed through an image, an artifice that does not imitate life so much as interpret it.

The chronicle is a permanent testing laboratory. It is the space of diffusion and contagion of a sensibility and a way of understanding the literary. It involves beauty, the conscious selection of language, and the creation of sensory images and symbols. It includes a mixture of foreign and local elements, of genres, of the arts, of democracy, and of epic. Nature, social and intimate reality, and the decadent pain of Parnassians and symbolists exist alongside faith in the future, cosmic harmony, liberalism, and the systematic doubt that already announces the arrival of amphibious modern man.

The chronicle is characterized by its insoluble hybridity, its condition of imperfection, its mobility, its social and institutional questioning, its syncretism and marginality. Most important, this period saw the development of a genre that is eminently Spanish American. The modernist chronicle constitutes the echo of an era, a time when the only certain and seizable knowledge is personal experience. From the age of the modernists to our own *fin de siècle*, we have moved dispersed among accelerated urban rhythms and a constant flow of information. Like the modernists, our strongest tradition is questioning, as we seek to find some beauty and harmony in the matter of our everyday lives.

Notes

1. The Logic of Literary Representation

1. This information is found in Max Henríquez Ureña's *Breve historia del modernismo* (Mexico City: Fondo de Cultura Económica, 1954), 156. Henríquez Ureña cites Darío's article "La literatura en Centroamérica," in which he refers to the Mexican writer Ricardo Contreras.

2. The term "animal laborans" belongs to Hannah Arendt and is cited by Rafael Gutiérrez Girardot in *Modernismo* (Barcelona: Montesinos, 1983), 88. Concerning the relationship between modernism and modernity, it is necessary to cite the skepticism of Roberto González Echevarría, for whom modern writers include Bolívar, Bello, and Esteban Echeverría ("El matadero"). In "Modernidad, modernismo y nueva narrativa: El recurso del método," *Inter-American Review of Bibliography* 30, no. 2 (1980): 157–58.

3. Angel Rama, "La dialéctica de la modernidad de José Martí," *Estudios martianos: Memoria del Seminario José Martí.* (Río Piedras: University of Puerto Rico, Editorial Universitaria, 1974), 129.

4. Unless otherwise noted, quotations of Martí are from *Obras completas* (Havana: Editora Nacional de Cuba, 1965–1975). The volume and page number will be indicated in the text in parentheses; volume number will be given in roman numerals for clarity. All translations and italics are mine unless otherwise noted.

5. Cf. Cecilia Tichi, "Instability, Waste, Efficiency," in *Shifting Gears: Technology, Literature, Culture in Modernist America* (Chapel Hill and London: University of North Carolina Press, 1987), 411–98.

6. A few biographical examples will suffice to illustrate this social mobility: Julián del Casal was the son of a sugar and slave plantation owner who struck hard times when the poet was old enough to begin his secondary studies. José Asunción Silva came from a landed aristocratic family, but his father was a merchant and the poet himself was forced to take on the decadent and bourgeois family business. Rubén Darío and Julio Herrera y Reissig received utterly impoverished inheritances. On the other hand, José Martí, famous for his words and his culture, holder of several university degrees, was the son of an uneducated Spaniard who worked for the Cuban police. At the other extreme is Leopoldo Lugones, who cultivated the pretensions of his Creole lineage and developed an extreme nationalism rooted in contempt for upstart immigrants. In terms of travel, Martí resided mostly in New York and Europe. Darío, like most modernists, visited Spain and Paris more than once. Paris was almost a requirement for writers of the time, although neither Herrera y Reissig nor Julián del Casal ever got there.

7. Claudio Véliz, *La tradición centralista de América Latina* (Barcelona: Ariel,

1984), 247, 213, 230. English edition: *The Centralist Tradition of Latin America*, trans. María Isabel Carreras and Ignacio Hierro (Princeton, N.J.: Princeton University Press, 1980).

8. José Luis Romero, *Latinoamérica: Las ciudades y las ideas*, 4th ed. (Mexico City: Siglo XXI, 1986), 252. English edition: *Latin America: Its Cities and Ideas*, trans. David William Foster (Boston: Unwin Hyman, 1989).

9. Jorge Mañach, *Martí, el apóstol* (Buenos Aires: Espasa-Calpe, 1942), 145.

10. Juan Bautista Alberdi observed: "If one had to compare the new spirit and the old spirit in Latin America, simple observation would lead to the conclusion that nineteenth-century Europe . . . was in the coastal provinces, and the past, more specifically, was in the inland cities. This can be understood because it is visible and tangible." In "Cartas quillotanas," *Obras completas,* vol. 4 (Buenos Aires: Imprenta de *La Tribuna Nacional*, 1886), 69.

11. See Marshall Berman, *All That Is Solid Melts into Air: The Experience of Modernity* (New York: Simon and Schuster, 1982), 15–36. Changes in the modes of production as well as the instability and broadening of the frontiers of knowledge made their marks on the system of writing. In *Las contradicciones del modernismo* (Mexico City: El Colegio de México, 1978), Noé Jitrik analyzes modernist texts as "semiotic machines," analogous to the new systems of production. Products are manufactured serially and poems take on rules of precision. Different and new series multiply. Capital and erudition accumulate. Technology arises as specialization and professionalization. Value is assigned through prices and adjectives. There is a struggle for consumerism in the market and spaces for reading. Past experiences are utilized. Inventions are imaginative and creativity original. Exhibitions in world fairs parallel magazine production. Jitrik also suggests that the transition from a system of writing to a mode of production took place most tangibly in journalism. Chronicles would then correspond to the modernist tendency to create new spaces of condensation in order to conceal antagonisms (110, 94–96).

12. For the shaping of patrician cities see Romero, 173 f.

13. In "León Bloy," *Los raros*, 4th ed., rev. and enl. (Barcelona: Casa Edit. Maucci 1907), 72.

14. Pierre Leroux, "De la loi de continuité qui unit le dix-huitième au dix-septième, *"Revue Encyclopédique*, 57 (March 1833), 480–81. This mention of Leroux is well-founded: like Martí, he proposed to take back the past to create a "current tradition" and affirm truths of the present. Furthermore, a great deal of his reflections about art have to do with notions of the future, symbols, purity of art, all of which are central aspects of modernist poetics. See Paul Bénichou, *Les temps des prophètes: Doctrines de l'age romantique* (Paris: Gallimard, 1977). Spanish edition: *El tiempo de los profetas: Doctrinas de la época romántica*, trans. A. Garzón del Camino (Mexico City: Fondo de Cultura Económica, 1984), 305–30.

15. See also Gerard Aching, *The Politics of Spanish American Modernismo: By Exquisite Design* (New York and London: Cambridge University Press, 1997); Oscar

Montero, *Erotismo y representación en Julián del Casal* (Amsterdam-Atlanta: Rodopi, 1993); Graciela Montaldo, "El terror letrado: sobre el modernismo latinoamericano," *Revista de Crítica Literaria Latinoamericana* 20, no. 40 (1984): 281–91.

16. Carlos Real de Azúa, "Modernismo e ideologías," offprint of *Punto de Vista* 9, no. 28 (November 1986): xxxi; it is a reprint of "El modernismo literario y las ideologías," *Escritura* 3 (Jan.–June 1977): 41–76.

17. Arturo Andrés Roig, *Teoría y crítica del pensamiento latinoamericano* (Mexico City: Fondo de Cultura Económica, 1981), chapter 13.

18. Cf. Roig, 261; Jürgen Habermas, *Historia crítica de la opinión pública*, trans. Domenech (Barcelona: Gustavo Gili, 1981), 201. English edition: *The Structural Transformation of the Public Sphere: An Inquiry into a Category of Bourgeois Society*, trans. Thomas Burger and Frederick Lawrence (Cambridge, Mass.: MIT Press, 1989). On the role of writers, see chapter 3.

19. *Sección constante: Historia, letras, biografía, curiosidades y ciencia*, ed. and intro. Pedro Grases (Caracas: Imprenta Nacional, 1955), 401.

20. A more extensive example of these ideas can be found in the following paragraph of the *Escenas norteamericanas:*

A kind of literature is called for that will announce and propagate the final and happy harmony of apparent contradictions . . . This literature will not only reveal a social state closer to perfection than any other so far, but, happily joining reason to grace, will provide Humanity with the religion that they have been waiting for since they knew the emptiness and sufficiency of their ancient creeds. (XIII, 134–35)

21. Charles Baudelaire, "Le peintre et la vie moderne" (1863). Cited by Octavio Paz, *Los hijos del limo. Del romanticismo a la vanguardia*, 3rd ed., rev. (Barcelona: Seix Barral, 1981), 131.

22. Max Weber, "La ciencia como profesión," *Ciencia y política*, trans. J. C. Torre (Buenos Aires: Centro Editor de América Latina, 1980). Related work in English: *Politics as Vocation* (Philadelphia: Fortress Press, 1972).

23. Peter Bürger notes in his article "Literary Institution and Modernization" that the process of rationalization "determines not only scientific and technical processes, but also moral decisions and the organization of everyday life." In *Poetics*, no. 12 (1983): 419.

24. The discussion about the true beginnings of modernity enthralled Europeans of the seventeenth century. See, for example, Gilbert Highet, *The Classical Tradition: Greek and Roman Influences on Western Literature* (New York and Oxford: Oxford University Press, 1985). On the identity of the New World: Tzvetan Todorov, *La conquète de l'Amérique: La question de l'autre* (Paris: Le Seuil, 1982). Enrique Dussel's position must be added to the debate: to him modernity is a European phenomenon in dialectic relation to its "non-European alterity" (in "Eurocentrism and Modernity [Introduction to the Frankfurt Lectures]," *Boundary 2: An International Journal of Literature and Culture* 20, no. 3 [Fall 1993]: 65–75). See also Guido A.

Podestá, "An Ethnographic Reproach to the Theory of the Avant-Garde: Modernity and Modernism in Latin America and the Harlem Renaissance," *Modern Language Quarterly* 57, no. 2, special issue edited by Doris Sommer (June 1966), 227–36.

25. Iván Schulman and Evelyn Picón Garfield, *Las entrañas del vacío: Ensayos sobre la modernidad hispanoamericana* (Mexico City: Cuadernos Americanos, 1984), 46. See also Schulman, "La modernización del modernismo hispanoamericano," in *Contextos: Literatura y sociedad latinoamericanas del sigo XIX*, ed. Schulman and Picón Garfield (Urbana: University of Illinois Press, 1991), 91–105.

26. *Recuerdos de provincia* (1843; reprint, Buenos Aires: Sopena, 1966), 92. Sarmiento was at once an editor, educator, and journalist. On the power of representation, see the reflections of Andrés Bello in relation to language and illustration. See especially his *Código civil de la República de Chile* in *Obras completas,* vol. 12 (Caracas: 1954). The Bello and Sarmiento case has been carefully investigated by Julio Ramos in "Contradicciones de la modernización literaria en América Latina: José Martí y la crónica modernista," Ph.D. diss., Princeton University, 1986, published as the influential *Desencuentros de la modernidad en América Latina* (Mexico City: Fondo de Cultura Económica, 1986). All the quotations from Ramos in this book correspond to the original version of his work, to which this analysis is indebted. Ramos has written other excellent studies related to this topic included in *Paradojas de la letra* (Caracas: eXcultura, 1996).

On the systematization of point of view from the site of power, see N. Poulantzas, *Estado, poder y socialismo*, trans. T. Claudin (Mexico City, Siglo XXI, 1979), 64 and forward. In Latin America: Angel Rama, *La ciudad letrada* (Hanover: Ediciones Del Norte, 1984); Josefina Ludmer, "Quién educa," in *Filología* (Buenos Aires: Sudamérica, 1988), 293–304. On the relationship between politics and literature, see the "partial" list compiled by Pedro Henríquez Ureña of almost thirty nineteenth-century writers who became presidents of their countries; in *Las corrientes literarias en la América Hispánica*, trans. J. Diez-Canedo (Mexico City: Fondo de Cultura Económica, 1949), 239.

27. Octavio Paz, *Poesía en movimiento* (Mexico City: Joaquín Mortiz, 1966), 123–29 (emphasis added).

28. Menéndez Pelayo, *Historia de los heterodoxos españoles*, vol. 7 (Buenos Aires: Espasa-Calpe, 1951), 118–25.

29. Octavio Paz, *Cuadrivio* (Mexico City: Joaquín Mortíz, 1965).

30. Pythagorism, Catholicism, and the occult were all decisive factors in these searches. See Ricardo Gullón, "Pitagorismo y modernismo," in *Nuevos asedios al modernismo*, ed. Iván Schulman (Madrid: Taurus, 1987), 86–107.

31. Michel Foucault, *The Order of Things: An Archeology of the Human Sciences* (New York: Random House, 1994), 251–52.

32. Ernest Renan, *L'avenir de la science: Pensées de 1948* (Paris: Calmann-Levy, 1890), 143. The relationship between modernists and Renan's postulates is rigorously analyzed by Aníbal González in his "Máquinas del tiempo: temporalidad y

narratividad en la crónica modernista," Ph.D. diss., Yale University, 1982). This work later appeared as *La crónica modernista hispanoamericana* (Madrid: J. Porrúa Tarranzas, 1982). Aníbal González also wrote one of the rare and lucid reference books on literature in Spanish American journalism, *Journalism and the Development of Spanish American Narrative* (Cambridge: Cambridge University Press, 1993).

33. Jorge Aguilar Mora, "El estilo como máscara," in *La divina pareja: Historia y mito en Octavio Paz* (Mexico City: Era, 1978), 96–97. Also Irving Zeitlin, *Ideología y teoría sociológica* (Buenos Aires: Amorrortu, 1976), 333, cited by Aguilar Mora.

34. Rubén Darío, *El canto errante,* in *Poesia,* ed. Ernesto Mejía Sánchez (Caracas: Biblioteca Ayacucho, 1977).

35. Fina García Marruz develops her idea about the textual "I" and the collective "I" in "Los versos de Martí" in *Temas martianos,* written in collaboration with Cintio Vitier (Puerto Rico: Huracán, 1981), 258.

36. *The Marx-Engels Reader,* ed. Robert C. Tucker (New York: Norton, 1978), 475–76.

37. Friedrich Nietzsche, *Más allá del bien y del mal,* trans. A. Sánchez Pascal, 5th ed. (Madrid: Alianza, 1979), 104.

38. Jürgen Habermas, "La modernidad inconclusa," *Vuelta* 54 (May 1981): 4.

39. Nilkas Luhman suggests a definition of the era that differentiates modernist discourse: "We live in a society without a summit and without a centre. The unity of society no longer comes out in this society . . . That is, no system can legitimate another." In "Representation of Society within Society," *Current Sociology* 35, no. 2 (1987): 105. The rationalizing discourse has shifted. But the seeds of this difficulty of representing unity can already be found in modernist texts, which had to call in rhetorical devices to tackle the problem.

40. Cited by Cornelius Castoriadis in *Les carrefours de labyrinthe* (Paris: Le Seuil, 1978), 10; translated into English as *Crossroads in the Labyrinth,* trans. Kate Soper and Martin H. Ryle (Cambridge: MIT Press, 1984).

41. Roland Barthes, *La chambre claire* (Paris: Le Seuil, 1980), 5. English edition, *Camera Lucida: Reflections on Photography,* trans. Richard Howard (New York: Hill and Wang, 1981).

42. For the boundaries on the modernism/modernity/contemporality relationship, I must note my debt to Jacques Leenhardt for his talk "La Querelle des Modernes et des Post-modernes" in the Centro de Estudios Avanzados of the University of Buenos Aires (1988). Although the topic there was the postmodernism of the Surrealists and Julio Cortázar, it was useful to appropriate notions of periods, especially the "period of suspicion" described by Nathalie Sarraute in 1938. Also Norbert Lechner's "Un desencanto llamado posmodernidad," *Punto de Vista* 11, no. 33 (Sept.–Dec. 1988): 26, and Marcel Gauchet, *Le désenchantement du monde* (Paris: Gallimard, 1985).

43. *Obras completas*, vol. 62 (Havana: Trópico, 1963–1965), 98. In order to abbreviate the references to this particular edition of Martí's work, they will be indicated in the text with the publisher, volume, and page.
44. Ernesto Laclau, *Política e ideología en la teoría marxista* (Madrid: Siglo XXI, 1986), 116. The English edition is *Politics and Ideology in Marxist Theory: Capitalism, Fascism, Populism* (London: NLB, 1977). Emphasis added.
45. The term "interpellation" is used in Althusser's sense: the function of any ideology is to constitute individuals as subjects, making them live their relation to the social structure as if that relation were autonomously determined (Laclau, 132).
46. Emmanuel Swedenborg, *Heaven and Hell* (New York: Pyramid Communications, Inc. 1976), 84.
47. The symbol is a break with classical language, which made the discourse's power apparent (Foucault, 302). Symbolism seeks equivocal discourse through an unusual word, that is, the object, the scenery, the myth, or the pairing of abstract and concrete characteristics that lack an evident relationship. These artifices are all attempts to transcend direct meaning and open up conjecture, in order to elevate the experience of both poet and reader to a level of multiple possibilities.
48. Manuel Gutiérrez Nájera, *Obras* (Mexico City: UNAM, 1959), 317.
49. The modernist novel cannot be reduced to an aesthetic formula: "it features the coexistence of new *fin de siècle* tendencies toward lyric narration and the true incorporation of nineteenth-century European realism and naturalism." Federico de Onís, "Tomás Carrasquilla, precursor de la novela americana moderna," in *La novela iberoamericana* (Albuquerque: University of New Mexico Press, 1952), 135.

2. The Writers' Role

1. See Tulio Halperín Dongui, *Historia contemporánea de América Latina*, 6th ed. (Madrid: Alianza, El Libro de Bolsillo, 1977), 289–355.
2. Véliz, 230. On the tertiary sector, see Richard M. Morse, "Recent Research on Latin American Urbanization: A Selective Survey with Comments," LARR 1 (Fall 1965): 38.
3. Marcos Kaplan, *Formación del estado nacional en América Latina* (Buenos Aires: Amorrortu, 1969), 183.
4. Pierre Bourdieu, *Campo del poder y campo intelectual*, trans. J. Dotti and M. T. Gramuglio (Buenos Aires: Folios, 1983), 14.
5. Jürgen Habermas, *L'espace public: Archéologie de la publicité comme dimension constitutive de la société bourgeoise*, trans. M. B. Launay (Paris: Payot, 1986), 184.
6. Dominick Lacapra, *Rethinking Intellectual History: Texts, Contexts, Language* (Ithaca and London: Cornell University Press, 1983), 159.
7. Pedro Henríquez Ureña, *Las corrientes literarias en América Hispánica*, trans.

Joaquín Diez Canedo (Mexico City: Fondo de Cultura Económica, 1949), 164–65. Emphasis added.

8. On the relationship between modernism and modernity, see the special issue "Para los siglos de José Martí," *Casa de las Américas* 35, no. 198 (Jan.–March 1995), especially the articles by Iván Schulman and Pedro Pablo Rodríguez.

9. Jürgen Habermas, *Historia crítica de la opinión pública: La transformación estructural de la vida pública*, trans. Domenech (Barcelona: Gustavo Gili, 1981), 201. English edition: *The Structural Transformation of the Public Sphere: An Inquiry into a Category of Bourgeois Society*, trans. Thomas Burger and Frederick Lawrence (Cambridge, Mass.: MIT Press, 1989). On the difference between the state superstructure and political practices as class struggle, see Nicos Poulantzas, *Pouvoir politique et classes sociales*, vol. 1 (Paris: Maspero, 1968); English edition: *Political Power and Social Classes*, trans. Timothy O'Hagan (London: Verso, 1975).

10. Letter from Rodó to Baldomero Sanín Cano, *Obras completas* (Madrid: Aguilar, 1957), 1374–75.

11. "This double perspective has yet to be evaluated: there was specialization, even to the degree of Darío's absorbing passion, and simultaneously general participation in the public forum, where one's personal destiny was often at risk . . ." (Angel Rama, *La ciudad letrada* [Hanover: Ediciones del Norte, 1984], 116).

12. See Rama, *Rubén Darío y el modernismo* (Caracas: Biblioteca Ayacucho, 1977), 45. See also Julio Romero, *Latinoamérica: Las ciudades y las ideas*, 4th ed. (Mexico City: Siglo XXI, 1986), English edition: *Latin America: Its Cities and Ideas*, trans. David William Foster (Boston: Unwin Hyman, 1989); and *El escritor y la industria cultural: El camino hacia la profesionalización*, ed. Jorge Rivera (Buenos Aires: Centro Editor de América Latina, 1980).

13. Eduardo Wilde, "Sobre poesía" (1870), compiled in *Tiempo perdido* (Buenos Aires: Jackson, n.d.)

14. "La atmósfera de los grandes diarios," in *Recuerdos literarios* (Buenos Aires: La Cultura Popular, 1937); in Rivera, ed., 75.

15. Habermas, *Problemas de legitimación en el capitalismo tardío* (Buenos Aires: Amorrortu, 1975), 99–110. English edition: *The Theory of Communicative Action*, trans., Thomas McCarthy (Boston: Beacon Press, 1984).

16. Rodó, *Ariel*, in *Obras completas*, ed. Emir Rodríguez Monegal (Madrid: Aguilar, 1957), 213.

17. Max Horkheimer, *Critical Theory: Selected Essays*, trans. Matthew J. O'Connell et al. (New York: Herder and Herder, 1972), 275.

18. José Asunción Silva, *Obra completa* (Medellin: Bedout, 1970): 227.

19. One text that modernists knew was Alejo García Moreno's 1870 translation of *Los mandamientos de la humanidad, o la vida moral en forma de catecismo según Krause, por G. Tibirghien, profesor de la Universidad Libre de Bruselas*, which states: "Art must work against depravity, not follow the current of things . . ." This

is cited by José A. Portuondo in *Martí: Escritor revolucionario* (Havana: Centro de Estudios Martianos y Editora Política, 1982), 15. See the previous chapter, as well as Pedro Aullón de Haro, "La construcción del pensamiento crítico literario moderno" in *Introducción a la crítica literaria actual* (Barcelona: Playor, 1984), 19–82; José Luis Gómez Martínez, "Krausismo, modernismo y ensayo" in *Nuevos asedios al modernismo*, 210–26; Pedro A. de Alarcón, "Discurso sobre la moral en el arte" in *Obras completas* (Madrid: Fax, 1950); Urbano González Serrano, "Consideraciones sobre el arte de la poesía" in *Krausismo: Estética y literatura*, comp. Juan López-Morillas (Barcelona: Labor, 1973), 207.

20. Gustave Flaubert, *Correspondance*, letter to Louise Colet, January 16, 1852 (cited in Bourdieu, 29). On *artepurismo* (purity of art), Gutiérrez Girardot maintains that its popularity with many writers had to do with their displacement as intellectuals in the new social order. Finding similarities between certain processes in European and Spanish American literature, many critics overlook important differences. They generalize about the function of the *fin de siècle* "intellectual" (the writer), and declare his lack of position within the class system; but many Spanish American writers in fact performed multiple functions, including political ones. Modernism cannot be considered an art that had no *raison d'être*, unless we limit the category of art to include only poetry as a production in and of itself, and examine this poetry according to strictly utilitarian principles. This discussion continues throughout the chapter (Rafael Gutiérrez Girardot, *Modernismo* [Barcelona: Montesinos, 1983]).

21. "Un poeta—Poesías de Francisco Sellén" (V, 191–92).

22. Portuondo, 15. The difference between Martí and other modernists is not in his will to style, but in the "ethical and aesthetic unity of the artist."

23. Manuel Pedro González and Iván Schulman, eds., *José Martí, esquema ideológico* (Mexico City: Cultura, 1951), 313.

24. Gutiérrez Nájera, "El arte y el materialismo," in *El modernismo visto por los modernistas*, ed. Ricardo Gullón (Barcelona: Guardarrama, 1980), 165.

25. A modernist inheritance, in this case, is the duality between a pure woman and a perverted one, as Rubén Darío would say. Martí's ideals of man "are much closer to Christ than to Rousseau," since the idea of a redeeming sacrifice is much more prominent in his work than the virtue of natural man (Fina García Marruz, in "José Martí," *Archivo de José Martí* 19–22 [Jan.–Dec. 1952]: 57). There are also studies such as Iván Schulman's on the use of symbols of the Holy Spirit and the Cross in *Símbolo y color en la obra de José Martí* (Madrid: Gredos, 1970).

The influence of Catholicism on Martí and the other modernists is undeniable. However, the attitude is anti-institutional because, as he wrote in a chronicle from New York for *La Nación* and *El Partido Liberal* in 1887, "what is degrading about Catholicism is the abuse of authority that the leaders of the church indulge in." Martí's work also bears the spirit of secularization: "The most demanding aspect of man's faith in religion is his faith in himself" (XI). This type of formulation coincides with the postulates of positivism as religion, in agreement with Auguste Comte and his successor Pierre Laffitte.

26. Sylvia Molloy, "Voracidad y solipsismo en la poesía de Rubén Darío," *Sin nombre* 11, no. 3 (Oct.–Dec. 1980): 9. See also Octavio Paz, *Cuadrivio* (Mexico City: Joaquín Mortiz, 1965).

27. Benjamin, Walter. "Paris, Capital of the Nineteenth Century," *Reflections,* trans. E. Jephcott (New York: Schocken Books, 1986), 154.

28. "The final condition of production is the reproduction of the condition of production." Louis Althusser, *Ideología y aparatos ideológicos de estado: Freud y Lacan* (1970, 1964), trans. A. J. Pla and J. Sazbón (Buenos Aires: Nueva Visión, 1988), 9.

29. "Programa" from the first issue of *Revista científica y literaria* (Buenos Aires: August 1883; in *Las revistas literarias,* ed. H. R. Lafleur and S. D. Provenzano (Buenos Aires: Centro Editor de América Latina, 1980), 19.

30. Cited by Adolfo Prieto in *El discurso criollista en la formación de la Argentina moderna* (Buenos Aires: Sudamericana, 1988), 50.

31. Criticism has revealed the role of both *gauchesca* and indigenist literature in promoting an aspiring national discourse. With some variations and exceptions, these literatures used models of the country—images or representations that they were supposed to copy and not re-create—to transmit a system of laws that was capable of establishing the interests of the elite among the masses. See, for example, Josefina Ludmer, "Quién educa"; Efraín Kristal, "Peruvian *Indigenismo* Narrative and the Political Debate about the Indian" (Ph.D. diss., Stanford University, 1985), published as *The Andes Viewed from the City: Literary and Political Discourse on the Indian in Peru 1848–1930* (New York: Peter Long, 1987).

32. Françoise Perús, *Literatura y sociedad en América Latina: El modernismo* (Mexico City: Siglo XXI, 1976), 64.

33. Juan Marinello, *Ensayos martianos* (Las Villas: Universidad Central de Las Villas, 1961), 172.

34. Jean Franco, *Historia de la literatura hispanoamericana,* 5th ed. (Barcelona: Ariel, 1983). English edition: *An Introduction to Spanish-American Literature,* 3rd ed. (Cambridge and New York: Cambridge University Press, 1994).

35. Here he reiterates the need for Americanism: "when the community [*pueblo*] into which one was born is not up to the level of its time, it is important to be a man of the time and of that [*pueblo*], but above all, a man of that [*pueblo*]."

36. *Obras del maestro,* in Gonzalo de Quesada y Aróstegui, XIII (Washington, Havana, Torino, Berlin: n.p., 1919), 389.

37. Letter to Borrero (May 25, 1893), *Prosas III* (Havana: Consejo Nacional de Cultura, 1963), 90.

38. Max Henríquez Ureña, *Breve historia del modernismo* (Mexico City: Fondo de Cultura Económica, 1954), 33.

39. Frederic Jameson, *The Political Unconscious: Narrative as a Socially Symbolic Act* (Ithaca, N.Y.: Cornell University Press, 1981), 94–95.

40. Jacques Lacan, *Le Seminaire libre I: Les Ecrits techniques de Freud* (Paris: Le Seuil, 1975); Fredric Jameson, "Imaginary and Symbolic in Lacan," *Yale French Studies* 55–56 (1977): 338–95. On the concepts of interpellation and ideology, see also: Catherine Belsey, *Critical Practice* (London and New York: Routledge, 1993); Ernesto Laclau, *Emancipación y diferencia* (Buenos Aires: Ariel, 1996).

41. This can also be read following the concept of allegory developed by Jameson in his polemical article, "Third-World Literature in the Era of Multinational Capitalism," *Social Text* 15 (Fall 1986): 65–88; or Barbara Johnson in *The Rhetoric of Empire: Colonial Discourse in Journalism, Travel Writing, and Imperial Administration,* ed. David Spurr. (Durham and London: Duke University Press, 1993): 63. See also Walter Benjamin, *Illuminations: Essays and Reflections,* ed. Hannah Arendt, trans. Harry Zohn (New York: Schocken Books, 1969).

42. Juan José Hernández Arregui, *Imperialismo y cultura* (Buenos Aires: Amerindia, 1957), 71–72.

43. See Gutiérrez Girardot, *Modernismo.* Also Gonzalo Sobejano, "Epater le bourgeois en la España literaria del 1900," in *Forma literaria y sensibilidad social* (Madrid: Gredos,1967), 1–48.

44. I cite Michael Lowy's definition from *Pour une sociologie des intellectuels révolutionaires* (Paris: Presses Universitaires de France, 1976), 17.

45. "Reification" is understood as the process of representation by which the results of human interaction appear as present, given, natural, and unchangeable. This process occludes their origin and the traces that could show them as a result of a theory, or a process designed to show precisely the absence of process or theory. See George Lukacs, "Reification and the Consciousness of the Proletariat," in *History and Class Consciousness,* trans. Rodney Livingston (Cambridge: MIT Press, 1971); Roland Barthes, *Mitologías,* trans. Héctor Schmucler (Mexico City: Siglo XXI, 1980).

46. This entire section of *The American Chronicles of José Martí* is indebted to the work of Carlos Real de Azúa.

47. See, for example, Noé Jitrik, "El sistema modernista o 'rubendariano'" in *Nuevos asedios al modernismo,* ed. Iván Schulman (Madrid: Taurus, 1987), 55.

48. Darío in "Dilucidaciones," prologue to *El canto errante.* Stimulating affirmations such as these always leave doubts in their wake. Helga Gallas maintains the following, in *Teoría marxista de la literatura,* trans. Ramón Alcalde (Buenos Aires: Siglo XXI, 1973):

> Is there a causal relationship between the emergence of these new forms and the state of awareness of the class in which they arose? . . . Or are modifications necessary stages in the process of evolution of artistic forms—a historical process that is not primarily determined by the state of awareness of a class (or of the authors that belong to it), but by factors relatively independent of ideology, such as the state of techniques of reproduction and communication, and the change, partly determined by these, in the structure and necessities of the public?

Further still: can these new forms be separated from the original structure of which they are a part, or are they determined by that structure and, for this reason, decadent? (17)

49. Fernando Ortiz, *Contrapunteo cubano del tabaco y del azúcar* (Havana: Jesús Montero, 1940); Angel Rama, *Transculturación narrativa en América Latina* (Mexico City: Siglo XXI, 1982).

3. The Emergence of the Chronicle

1. W. Sombart, *Der Bourgeois*, quoted by Habermas in *The Structural Transformation of the Public Sphere: An Inquiry into a Category of Bourgeois Society*, 217.

2. Sarmiento, "La cultura del pueblo: El diarismo," *El Nacional*, published in two parts, May 15 and 29, 1849. Reproduced in *Polémica literaria* (Buenos Aires: Cartago, 1933), 13. The first italics are in the original text.

3. For a similar analysis of the function of the press, see J. A. Saco, *La vagancia en Cuba* (Havana: Cuadernos de Cultura, 1946), 85–87.

4. *La Nación* (February 2, 1883): 1. I use this Argentine newspaper as the central axis of my analysis of journalism because it was a nucleus for the great modernist voices as well as one of the newspapers of greatest influence and innovative drive in Spanish America. The observations about the front page were developed during a study of the original material (published between 1875 and 1895), carried out over several months in the archives of *La Nación* in the Hemeroteca de la Biblioteca Nacional de Buenos Aires.

   In the analysis that occupies the first part of this chapter I have used the following references: José Acosta Montoro, *Periodismo y literatura*, vol. 1 (Madrid: Guardarrama, 1973); Beatriz Alvarez et al., *Artes y letras en "La Nación" de Buenos Aires (1870–1899)* (Buenos Aires: Fondo Nacional de las Artes, 1968); Oscar Beltrán, *Historia del periodismo argentino* (Buenos Aires: Perlado, 1943); Camila Henríquez Ureña et al., *El periodismo en José Martí* (Havana: Orbe, 1977); Oksana María Sirko, "La crónica modernista en sus inicios: José Martí y Manuel Gutiérrez Nájera," in *Estudios críticos sobre la prosa modernista hispanoamericana*, ed. José Oviedo Jiménez (New York: Eliseo Torres & Sons, 1975); Gonzalo de Quesada y Miranda, *Martí periodista* (Havana: Bouza y Cía, 1929); Fryda Weber, "Martí en *La Nación* de Buenos Aires," *Archivo José Martí: Número del Centenario* (Havana: Ministerio de Educación, 1953), 458–82. The works on the modernist chronicle already cited were also of great use, especially those by Julio Ramos and Aníbal González; see also other cited works by Prieto and Rivera.

5. Gutiérrez Nájera, *Escritos ineditos* (Columbia: University of Missouri Press, 1972), 55.

6. This information was recovered by Alfred Veiravé, "Cuentos de amor, de locura y

de muerte (1917). El almohadón de plumas. Lo ficticio y lo real," in *Aproxima-ciones a Horacio Quiroga*, ed. Angel Flores (Caracas: Monte Avila, 1976), 209–14.

7. Examples of serialized fiction: "La madre de Enrique IV. El casamiento de Juana de Albert," by the Baron A. de Ruble, Paris, 1887 (January 29, 1881); "Don Juan Solo," by Ortega Munilla (February 1881); "El Bichwess. Cuento de un eclesiástico," by Hugo Conway (July 29, 1885); "Corazón y ciencia," by Wilkie Collins (September 1885). Even Aben Xoar, the most common signature of the previous period—that of the *costumbrista* conversations—was totally displaced in the eighties.

8. The story "El falso artista," for example, bears only the initials "J. P." as signature. It does not occupy the lower space of the front page traditionally dedicated to seri-alized novels, but rather appears in the columns like the rest of the material (Feb-ruary 20, 1881). "La leyenda de la ciencia" is a news story signed by Emilio Cas-telar, but the only real difference between the layout of this text and "El falso artista" is the length of the material itself.

9. This study was carried out by consulting the microfilm collection of the Hemerot-eca of the Biblioteca Nacional de Caracas.

10. This section was so extensive that it sometimes occupied the entire front page for several issues. This happened, for example, with an eight-issue piece on General José Antonio Sucre in 1881.

11. The advertisements also convey the cosmopolitanism that was imposed in Caracas at the time. In the January 31, 1881, issue, we read of "the true elixir of Dr. Guillié," a textile company that offers a "magnificent wick, not rivaled even by the famous American one," a still factory, machines to prepare coffee, and phenic acid syrup for the stomach. Not to mention Doctor Radway's remedies: "marvels of modern chemistry; the fast relief of Dr. Radway, Radway's sarsaparilla. Regulating Radway pills." Also lithium salts, a surgeon, Quinina Larroche elixir, houses for sale, Gri-meult de Cadet injections, hats, Reuter syrup, ylang yling from Manila, "The King of Perfumes," curative soap from Reuter, Barry Ivory for teeth, English hardware, Polene and Whitman chemical products, and Oriza soap from Paris.

12. See Raimundo Lida, introduction, "Los cuentos de Rubén Darío," in *Rubén Darío: Cuentos completos*, ed. Ernesto Mejía Sánchez (Mexico City: Fondo de Cultura Económica, 1950). Rama adds: "The series of eight chronicles that he wrote for *El Heraldo* of *Valparaíso* contains the best pages of prose that Darío wrote during his Chilean period. The one published on March 10, 1888, on the death of the German emperor, can only be compared to texts as famous as "El velo de la reina Mab," "El rey burgués," or "La canción del oro." In Rama, *Rubén Darío y el modernismo* (Caracas: Universidad Central de Venezuela, 1970), 79.

13. Ernesto, "Notas literarias: el periodismo y las letras," *La Nación* (November 30, 1889): 1. The author's last name is not given.

14. Cited in Gonzalo de Quesada y Miranda, *Martí periodista*, 97. The quotations that follow are from pages 98 and 99.

15. Letter from Mitre to Martí (cited in Quesada y Miranda, 105).

16. Antonio Castro Leal, "Prólogo," to Luis G. Urbina, *Cuentos vividos y crónicas soñadas* (Mexico City: Porrada, 1971), ix.

17. See Raymond Williams, *Communications* (Harmondsworth: Penguin Books, 1969).

18. Ernesto Quesada, "El periodismo argentino," *Nueva revista* (Buenos Aires) 9 (1883).

19. Julián del Casal, *Crónicas habaneras*, comp. A. Augier (Las Villas: Universidad Central de Las Villas, 1963), 287–88.

20. Darío in "La enfermedad del diario," *Escritos inéditos*, ed. E. K. Mapes (New York: Instituto de Las Españas, 1958), 51. Emphasis added.

21. Manuel Gutiérrez Nájera, *Crónicas de "Puck," Obras inéditas*, ed. E. K. Mapes (New York: Instituto de las Españas en Estados Unidos, 1939), 7.

22. Darío, *Autobiografía* (Buenos Aires: Marymar, 1976), 63.

23. Quoted in Cintio Vitier and Fina García Marruz, *Temas martianos* (Puerto Rico: Huracán, 1981), 317–18.

24. The last statement is from José Emilio Pacheco, "Prólogo" to the anthology *Poesía modernista*, ed. Pacheco (Mexico: SEP-UNAM, 1982), 2. He says in addition that "like poetry, journalism was searching for something new," and it "transformed literature by creating new genres."

25. The texts cited from the two issues of the *Revista Venezolana* that Martí edited are faithful copies of the originals, which are reproduced on microfilm by the Hemeroteca of the Biblioteca Nacional de Caracas. The italics are mine: the first show how the urgencies of journalism were not always at odds with a "polished and elegant" style. The next quotations are from "El carácter de la *Revista Venezolana*," July 15, 1881.

26. "Propósitos," *Revista Venezolana*, July 1, 1881.

27. She adds two observations. The first is that the *croniqueurs*, in order to differentiate themselves from the "common *reporters*," limited themselves to a kind of press with a "doctrinal character, French style, aimed at a more select audience," instead of concentrating on information "based on news and sensation, American-style, aimed at recently formed middle sectors." The second observation is that "the compartmentalization of each activity—and each readership—is never that clean: we must not forget that the press was the mouthpiece of criticism and of the fame of a certain Darío." In Françoise Perús, *Literatura y sociedad en América Latina: El modernismo* (Mexico: Siglo XXI, 1976), 86–88.

28. Cited in Félix Lizaso, *Martí, místico del deber* (Buenos Aires: Losada, 1940), 233.

29. Joaquín V. González, "El periodismo y la literatura," *Obras completas,* vol. 18 (Universidad Nacional de la Plata, 1936), 344.

30. Manuel González Prada, "Nuestro periodismo," in *Horas de lucha* (Callao: Lux, 1924), 113.

31. The explanation that Juan Valera gave in 1893 is useful, quoted by Acosta Montoro, 83–84:

Being a journalist is, without a doubt, a profession or vocation, like being an engineer, a lawyer, or a doctor. It is thus evident that the journalist must be a literato of a determined class . . . What sets a journalist apart from any other writer has little or nothing to do with literature. The distinction that gives him his own character is independent of literature. Literati who write frequently or even daily large fold-outs that are spread among the public, sometimes by the hundreds of thousands, are called journalists.

32. Roland Barthes, *Ensayos críticos*, trans. Carlos Pujol (Barcelona: Seix Barral, 1976), 184–85. English edition: *Critical Essays*, trans. Richard Howard (Evanston, Ill.: Northwestern University Press, 1972).

33. Walter Benjamin, "The Author as Producer," in *Reflections*, ed. Peter Demetz, trans. Edmund Jephcott (New York: Schocken Books, 1986), 99.

34. Peter Bürger, *Theory of the Avant-Garde*, trans. M. Shaw (Minneapolis: University of Minnesota Press, 1984), 59.

35. *Obras completas* I (Havana: Lex, 1946), 823.

36. Cintio Vitier and Fina García Marruz, *Temas martianos,* 194–95.

37. Ibid.

38. Walter Benjamin, "The Artist as Producer," 23.

39. Boris Arbatov, *Arte y producción: El programa del productivismo*, trans. José Fernández Sánchez (Madrid: Comunicación, Serie B, 1973).

40. John Dewey, *Art as Experience* (New York: Capricorn Books, Putnam, 1958), 5.

41. Castoriardis, 16–17. Iván Schulman maintains that the Spanish American literary rebirth begins with the prose of José Martí and Manuel Gutiérrez Nájera, who, between 1875 and 1882, cultivated very different innovative forms of expression. "Nájera's prose was of patent French descent, revealing the presence of symbolism, Parnassianism, impressionism, and expressionism; Martí's incorporated the same influences into a structure of Hispanic origin. Consequently, it is in this so unjustly brushed-aside prose that the modernist aesthetic takes form." "Reflexiones en torno a la definición del modernismo," *Estudios críticos sobre el modernismo*, ed. Homero Castillo (Madrid: Gredos, 1968), 329.

42. The information is from Juan Beneyto, *"Mass Communications": Un panorama de los medios de información en la sociedad moderna* (Madrid: Instituto de Estudios Políticos, 1957), 81.

43. On the first English chroniclers, Addison and Steele, see George Weil, *El diario: Historia y función de la prensa periodística* (Mexico: Fondo de Cultura Económica, 1941), 10, 52. On the French, among whom one of the best was undoubtedly Balzac, see Margarite Ucelay da Cal, *Los españoles pintados por sí mismos (1843–1844): Estudio de un género costumbrista* (Mexico City: El Colegio de México, 1951), 164–66.

44. "The first of the great operations of discipline is, then, the constitution of 'tableaux

vivants' that transform the confused, useless, or dangerous multitudes into ordered multiplicities." He goes on to say that the painting or tableau, in the eighteenth century, is at once a technique of power and a procedure of knowledge. It is a question of organizing what is multiple, of obtaining an instrument to dominate it. An "order" must be imposed. Michel Foucault, *Vigilar y castigar: Nacimiento de la prisión*, 8th ed. (1973), trans. A. Garzón del Camino (Mexico City: Siglo XXI, 1983), 152. English edition: *Discipline and Punish: The Birth of the Prison*, trans. Alan Sheridan (New York: Vintage Books, 1977).

45. *Histoire générale de la presse française*, vol. 2 (Paris: Presse Universitaires de France, 1969), 298–302. Auguste Villemont also gave an excellent definition in *Le Figaro* in 1945: "Une chronique étant l'éxpression de la société vous voyez c'ici les conséquences. Dans ce métier, ce que es plus essentiel que l'initiative de l'esprit c'est son aptitude a saisir les travers et les ridicules de son temps, une certaine intuition de ce que est plaisant de sa nature, une probité de caractère qui permet de d'éffleurer les choses sans blesser les hommes (*ludere, non laedere*), et par-dessus tout, l'art de depouiller le mouvement de contemporain de ses detritus, pour en donner l'expression en un mot." Cited by Aníbal González-Pérez, *La crónica modernista hispanoamericana* (Madrid: J. Porrúa Tarranzas, 1982), 86–87.

46. Cited by Boyd G. Carter in "Estudio preliminar," *Divagaciones y fantasías: Crónicas de Manuel Gutiérrez Nájera* (Mexico City: SepSetentas, 1974), 14.

47. The next chapter of this book is dedicated to the exhaustive study of José Martí's American chronicles in their different modalities. Here I only point out their journalistic "relations."

48. Carlos Monsiváis, *A ustedes les consta: Antología de la crónica en México*, 2nd ed. (Mexico City: Era, 1981), 21–26.

49. Ricardo Palma, *Cien tradiciones peruanas*, ed. José Miguel Oviedo (Caracas: Biblioteca Ayacucho, 1977). All quotations come from this edition and are indicated in the text in parentheses.

50. Sarmiento, *Viajes por Europa, Africa y América* (1849), in *Viajes*, ed. Alberto Palcos (Buenos Aires: Hacette, n.d.), 11.

51. *Costumbristas cubanos del siglo XIX*, comp. Salvador Bueno (Caracas: Biblioteca Ayacucho, 1985). Quintín Suzarte uses the word "goajiro" for *guajiro*.

52. Monsiváis, 108. All the Mexican chronicles mentioned here appear in this anthology.

53. In *América: la lucha por la libertad*, ed. Manuel Maldonado Denis (Mexico City: Siglo XXI, 1980), 65–80.

54. The opposition between old and new is a common motif in regionalist literature; for example: "Every nation should have its own special character. Is there national life without local literature? . . . Why should we *live the old European life in the new American land*?" (VI, 227).

55. See Leonard J. Davis, "A Social History of Fact and Fiction: Authorial Disavowal

in the Early English Novel," in *Literature and Society*, ed. Edward W. Said (Baltimore: Johns Hopkins University Press, 1980), 124 f.

56. Cited by Antonio Gómez Alfaro: "Comunicación, periodismo, literatura," *Gaceta de la prensa* 126 (Madrid 1960): 8. Charles Dana's thoughts on journalism can be added to this: "The first thing which an editor must look for is news. By news I mean everything that occurs, everything which is of human interest. I have always felt that whatever the divine Providence permitted to occur I was not too proud to report." Cited in Sidney Kobre, *Development of American Journalism* (Iowa: W. H. C. Brown Company, 1969), 368.

57. Y. Tinianov, *El problema de la lengua ética* (Buenos Aires: Siglo XXI, 1972); Oswald Ducrot and Tzvetan Todorov, *Encyclopedic Dictionary of the Sciences of Language*, trans. Catherine Porter (Baltimore: Johns Hopkins University Press, 1979).

58. Jonathan Culler, *La poética estructuralista: El estructuralismo, la lingüística y el estudio de la literatura*, trans. Carlos Manzano (Barcelona: Anagrama, 1980), 230. Related work in English: *Structuralist Poetics: Structuralism, Linguistics, and the Study of Literature* (Ithaca, N.Y.: Cornell University Press, 1975).

59. Here I follow the suggestions of Northrop Frye, *The Anatomy of Criticism: Four Essays* (New York: Athenaeum, 1965).

60. If we take Jakobson's model for categorizing language, we come to the following conclusions about the modernist chronicle: the factors of the originator, context, code, receiver, message, and contact, with their respective derived functions (the emotive, connotative, phatic, metalinguistic, referential, and poetic) present a particular set of balances and coexistences where the poetic function (verbal art as dominant) is not less important than the referential, for example. It would be interesting to examine this phenomenon and that of poetic prose itself, in light of Jakobson's famous postulate that the poetic function projects the beginning of equivalence of the axis of selection to the axis of combination. See Roman Jakobson, *On Language*, ed. Linda R. Waugh and Monique Monville-Burston (Cambridge, Mass.: Harvard University Press, 1990).

61. P. N. Medvedev or M. M. Bakhtin, "The Elements of the Artistic Construction," *The Formal Method in Literary Scholarship: A Critical Introduction to Sociological Poetics*, trans. Albert J. Wehrle (Baltimore: Johns Hopkins University Press, 1978), 120–35.

62. Richard Ohman, "Politics and Genre in Nonfiction Prose," *New Literary History* 11, no. 2 (Winter 1980): 243.

4. Writing the Present

1. Temporality should not be understood in the structuralist sense of temporal and spatial order. Both terms are used here in their most common sense, with relation

to the external referent rather than the internal elements of the text: temporality (the relationship with time as awareness of history, the present and the future, and what is fleeting and secular); spatiality (that which pertains or refers to a determined space: a region, a country, a continent). For the structuralist definition see Oswald Ducrot and Tzetvan Todorov, *Encyclopedic Dictionary of the Sciences of Language,* trans. Catherine Porter (Baltimore: Johns Hopkins University Press, 1994).

Concerning the aesthetic proposals of Martí's chronicles, it is possible to find reflections of his personal activism in the cause of Cuban liberation in his texts. This commitment was so central to Martí that it obviously had to influence his system of representation. The qualities of leadership that suffuse the enunciating subject in his texts has as much to do with inheritance from the European Enlightenment as with the concrete situation of Cuba and Puerto Rico, stopped in their historical processes compared to the rest of the continent. Martí the writer was the founder of an aesthetic that, without a doubt, changed the system of representation of the Latin American world, but his role as a hero of Cuban independence has clouded the magnitude of Martí's contribution to literature. This book deliberately excludes other considerations of Martí's leadership in order to concentrate on the construction of his poetics as a totality. For this reason, the large body of studies on the political figure of José Martí are not included here, excepting those that truly shed light on his literature. What this chapter's comparison of Martí's work with that of other contemporaneous authors does show is the striking heterogeneity of ways in which writing is used to construct the Nation.

2. Cintio Vitier and Fina García Marruz, *Temas martianos* (Puerto Rico: Huracán, 1981), 199.

3. Martí's North American experience is also discussed in the following chapter.

4. Edwin Emery, *The Press and America: An Interpretive History of the Mass Media* (Englewood Cliffs, N.J.: Prentice Hall, Inc., 1972), 267.

5. "The reporters constituted a galaxy of stars who could extract dramatic, tragic, humorous, and above all, human elements from an event . . . *The Sun* training they received led them later into the writing of novels and plays and of articles for magazines." Sidney Kobre, *Development of American Journalism* (Iowa: W. H. C. Brown Company, 1969), 368.

6. Frank M. O'Brien, *The Story of "The Sun"* (New York: D. Appleton and Company, 1928), 151.

7. Jacob Riis, *How the Other Half Lives* (1890; reprint, New York: Hill and Wang, 1957); *Jacob Riis Revisited,* ed. Francisco Cordasco (New York: Doubleday, 1968).

8. Michael Schudson, *Discovering the News: A Social History of American Newspapers* (New York: Basic Books, 1978), 64.

9. From Iván Schulman's anthology, *Ismaelillo, Versos libres, Versos sencillos* (Madrid: Cátedra, 1982), 95.

10. This sentence by Jorge Luis Borges is from an analysis of the poetry of Walt

Whitman, whom he describes as "the first Atlas who tried to win that struggle and took the world on his shoulders" (*Inquisiciones* [Buenos Aires: Proa, 1925], 91). What is interesting is not Borges' error in dating the origin of *Leaves of Grass* (the definitive version was produced in 1885), but his observation that the textual "I" altered the poetic system of representation.

As we will see in this chapter, the innovations that Martí introduces in his chronicles and poetry are synchronic with those of other creators, who saw themselves as new men and mouthpieces of modernity. This makes it difficult to determine who was truly the first to formulate each aesthetic proposal. Without trying to attribute absolute originality to Martí, however—he could have read Whitman in earlier versions, even though the latter was not yet well known as a poet—it is remarkable that each element he uses to construct his chronicles breaks with the traditional concept of writing, and, therefore, with accepted ways of perceiving reality itself.

11. Luis Lorenzo-Rivero, in his *Larra y Sarmiento* (Madrid: Guadarrama, 1968), finds oratorical devices in the texts of these two authors, whom he considers without a doubt the greatest in Spanish American newspaper writing at that time. He observes the following about Larra: "The public read independent articles and the object of *Fígaro* was to speak the truth to each one of those isolated readers. But he frequently wrote as if they were in front of him and he were speaking to them . . . Sarmiento also writes as if in the presence of his readers, addressing the public as if in a speech, irrupting forcefully, transmitting his emotions in questions and exclamations, dominated by passion and irrepressible impulse" (215). He adds that both authors use questions and exclamations as devices, as well as double progressive enumeration, and such remarkable visual descriptions of the characters' movements and emotions "that the reader has the sensation of seeing their actions" (212). See Luis Alvarez, *Estrofa, imagen, fundación: La oratoria de José Martí* (Havana: Casa de las Américas/Cocultura, 1995). This study received the Premio Extraordinario for scholarship on José Martí from Casa de las Américas that year.

12. On the novelty of Martí's writing see also Roberto Fernández Retamar, *Nuestra América: Cien años y otros acercamientos a Martí* (Havana: Si-Mar, 1995).

13. "Mis recuerdos de Martí," *Revista Cubana* 29 (July 1951–Dec. 1952): 48. This entire issue of the magazine is dedicated to testimonies of people who knew Martí. It includes poignant observations that confirm the relationship between oratory and writing in Martí's texts, such as those by Domingo Estrada (112–13) and Lincoln de Zayas (148). This issue of *Revista Cubana* is an invaluable measure of the innovative impact of Martí's work on his contemporaries, a basic criterion to consider in gauging the innovative value of an author.

14. "Martí pensador," in *Antología crítica de José Martí*, ed. Manuel Pedro González (Mexico City: Cultura, 1960), 534.

15. For these thinkers, the image contained an idea, a thought that was itself an action. Each had his own variation on the goal of working with power-ideas or images

that could persuade or make people see themselves or reality in a different way. They would then be able to choose between various options without mechanically repeating conventions. "The greatness of one would bring on the greatness of another," wrote Alfred Fouillé in *Libertad y determinismo*, trans. Luis Alcalá-Zamora y Castillo (Buenos Aires: La España Moderna, n.d.), 98 f. Form could break the mental cliché: on this point the modernists agreed.

Again it is difficult to know where Martí gathers the seeds of his ideas. Writers of the American Renaissance—Emerson and Whitman among them—also developed ideas in which the United States was seen as utopian, a reaction against Puritan ideas of the tragic fallibility of man. "To think is to act" are not Fouillé's words, but they could be. They were written by Emerson, as were "This power is in the image because this power is in Nature" (cited in F. O. Mathiessen, *The American Renaissance: Art and Expression in the Age of Emerson and Whitman* [New York: Oxford University Press, 1946], 21, 42). They all worked with praise, convinced of harmony, and of the need to teach men the new religion. But the sublime is also the quest of Calderón and the Spanish *Krausistas*; and the same can be said for the Greek rhetoricians such as Longinus, whose strategies are also present in Martí's chronicles.

16. "All that is beautiful, good, true, and possesses analogous qualities, is Divine, as is that which feeds and fortifies the winds of the soul." In Plato, "Fedro o el amor," *Diálogos* (Mexico City: Porrúa, 1981), 637. On enthusiasm, ecstasy, delirium inspired by the divine, and art, see 637–56. English edition: "Phaedrus" in *Dialogues*, trans. Benjamin Jowett (Oxford: Clarendon Press, 1969).

17. Longinus, *De lo sublime* (Buenos Aires: Aguilar, 1980), 28, 61. English edition: *On the Sublime,* trans. D. A. Russell (Oxford: Clarendon Press, 1965). Martí advocated praise instead of censure and explains his position quite simply in a letter to Manuel Mercado: "Everyone has their own defects; but qualities, how many have those?" (XX, 135). For Martí, as for the romantics, the educating function of written speech was still important.

On this subject see also Josef Pieper, *Enthusiasm and Divine Madness* (New York: Harcourt, Brace & World, Inc., 1964), and *Love and Inspiration: A Study of Plato's Phaedrus* (London: Faber and Faber: 1964); George Kennedy, *The Art of Persuasion in Greece* (Princeton, N.J.: Princeton University Press, 1963); Alfonso Reyes: "La antigua retórica" in *Obras completas*, vol. 13 (Mexico City: Fondo de Cultura Económica, 1961), 349–587; and, of course, Aristotle, *El arte de la retórica* (Buenos Aires: Eudeba, 1979); *The Art of Rhetoric*, trans. H. C. Lawson-Tancred (London and New York: Penguin Books, 1991).

18. See José Ballón, *Autonomía cultural americana: Emerson y Martí* (Madrid: Pliegos, 1986).

19. Punctuation marks denote intonation in Martí's texts. He wanted to create additional ones, such as the minor comma, the reading accent, and the minor dash (XXI, 338). On neologisms, see Alan M. Gordon's study, "Verbo-Creation in the

Works of José Martí," Ph.D. diss., Harvard University, 1956; also Manuel Pedro González, "José Martí: Jerarca del modernismo," in *Miscelánea de estudios dedicados al Doctor Fernando Ortiz por sus discípulos, colegas y amigos* (Havana: 1956), 740–41. On the point in common between Martí and Baltazar Gracián, see Manuel Pedro González and Iván Schulman, *Martí, Darío y el modernismo*, 143. From a more general standpoint, see also Juan Marinello, "Sobre Martí escritor: La españolidad literaria de José Martí," in *Vida y pensamiento de Martí* (Havana: Municipio de La Habana, 1942), 159–252. This analysis of oratorical techniques has been applied to *OC*, XIII. To avoid repetition, pagination will appear within the text in parentheses at the end of each quotation.

20. On the universal language of modern poetry see Hans Magnus Enzenberger, *Detalles* (Barcelona: Anagrama, 1969). Angel Rama claimed that Martí "clearly understood that all of humanity had been put in the same boat together for the first time in the history of the planet, and that the expansive characteristics of the scientific and technical civilizations of the nineteenth century made impossible any attempt at seclusion or segregation" ("La dialéctica de la modernidad en José Martí" [Memoria sobre el Seminario de José Martí, 1974], *Estudios martianos* [Rio Piedras: Universidad de Puerto Rico, Editorial Universitaria, 1974]).

21. According to Manuel Pedro González, Martí uses two stylistic devices: the baroque style and the apothegm style. *José Martí en el octogésimo aniversario de la iniciación modernista, 1882–1962* (Caracas: Biblioteca Venezolana de la Cultura, 1962), 47.

22. Vitier and García Marruz find a "natural baroquism" in Martí's work. "This is the Martí of *Versos libres*: darkness and flames, foam and volcanic matter, the abrupt and distinguished, fright, tenderness and fury, all searching in the battle of opposites and the agonies of the soul, for the painful unity of destiny" (Cintio Vitier and Fina García Marruz, *Temas martianos* [Puerto Rico: Huracán, 1981], 161).

23. Baldomero Sanín Cano, *El oficio del lector*, ed. Juan Gustavo Cobo Borda (Caracas: Biblioteca Ayacucho 48, 1978), 20.

24. In fact, they both inherit Emersonian transcendentalism. Martí's analysis of Whitman's texts is not, in essence, a discovery, but an admiring confirmation of what he himself believed about the new poetics. A clear fact distinguished Whitman from the transcendentalists, Martí included: Whitman managed to resolve the dichotomy between the material and the ideal; in his poems body and soul experience a single desire. On the other hand, Martí's Catholic and romantic inheritances prevent him from reaching this resolution. He dedicated very few lines in "Whitman" to the eroticism of *Leaves of Grass*. Martí's division is notorious in his treatment of women, who are stereotypically represented as mother or lover throughout his work. On Walt Whitman, see Mathiessen, 518–624. A reading useful in rethinking both authors is Sylvia Molloy, "His America, Our America: Martí Reads Whitman," *Modern Language Quarterly: A Journal of Literary History* 57, no. 2 (June 1996): 369–79.

25. In "Nuestro periodismo," 113.
26. "Les dernières notes de voyage de José Martí. Quelques remarques sur leur style," *Les Langues Neolatines*, n. 161, 1962 (cited in Vitier and García Marruz, 132–33). Some of the ideas developed here are based on Vitier and García Marruz's work.
27. On specific symbols in Martí's work, see Iván Schulman, "El simbolismo de José Martí: Teoría y lenguaje,"*Inti: Revista de cultura Hispánica et Luso-Brasilera* 8 (1978): 7–28.
28. Cited in Iván Schulman, *Génesis del modernismo: Martí, Nájera, Silva, Casal* (Mexico City: El Colegio de México; Washington University Press, 1966), 35.
29. Baldomero Sanín Cano, *El oficio de lector* (Caracas: Biblioteca Ayacucho, vol. 48, n.d.), 152.
30. See Graciela García Marruz, "El expresionismo en la prosa de José Martí," *Estudios críticos sobre la prosa modernista hispanoamericana*, ed. José Oviedo Jiménez (New York: Eliseo Torres & Sons, 1975), 35–55.
31. This exalted and pained imagination, however, is also capable of submitting itself to a rigorous architecture in which the mathematics of language makes each word necessary. Martí gives a vivid account of the Chicago anarchists:
    "Men and Women of my beloved America," Parsons begins to say. A signal, a noise, and the platform gives way. The four bodies fall in the air for the first time, spinning and bumping each other. Parsons has died on impact, turns, stops; Fischer swings, trembles, wants to cut the noose from his whole neck, stretches and recoils his legs, and dies; Engel rocks in his floating smock, his chest rises and falls like the tide and he suffocates; Spies, in a frightful dance, hangs spinning like a bag of grimaces, curls up, rises sideways, his knees against his forehead, raises one leg, extends them both, shakes his arms, patters, and finally expires, his neck broken forwards, bowing his head at the spectators. (XI, 355)
32. In this essay, Rama claims that Martí and Rimbaud "are both the fathers of modernity, one on each side of the Atlantic. They practically register on the same dates the first exact contemporaneous occurrence on the cultural clocks of Europe and America" (Angel Rama, "La dialéctica de la modernidad en José Martí, *Estudios martianos* [Rio Piedras: Universidad de Puerto Rico, Editorial Universitaria], 197).
33. Sarmiento, "La crítica teatral," *Obras completas*, vol. 1 (Buenos Aires: Luz del Día, 1948), 151.
34. Luis Monguió, *Estudios sobre literatura hispanoamericana y española* (Mexico City: Studium, 1958), 20–21.
35. I owe this information to González and Schulman, *Martí, Darío y el modernismo* 119–23.
36. *Sound Patterns in a Poem of José Martí* (Salt Lake City: Damuir Press, 1975), 34.
37. Walter Ong, "A Dialectic of Annual and Objective Correlatives," in *Perspectives on Poetry*, ed. J. L. Calderwood and H. E. Toliver (New York: Oxford University Press, 1968), 121.

38. Harold Bloom, *The Anxiety of Influence: A Theory of Poetry* (New York: Oxford University Press, 1997), 26.

39. These definitions correspond to those given by María Moliner in her *Diccionario del uso del español* (Madrid: Gredos, 1984). The term "syncretism" was accepted by the Spanish Royal Academy as a philosophical term in 1834, as J. Corominas and J. A. Pascual attest in the *Diccionario crítico etimológico castellano e hispánico* (Madrid: Gredos, 1983). These data corroborate our belief that this idea was deeply rooted in the thinking of the time.

40. Martí advocated the betterment of mankind through willingness and sacrifice, liberty and respect for man as such. He advocated man in his social right, not according to ethnicity, or historical conditions or separations. It is true that he engaged in impressionist frescoes, which were portraits of national "types." He did indeed believe that societies have "particular active characters, ideas and habits, expansion and acquisition, vanity and avarice" (in *Nuestra América* [Caracas: Biblioteca Ayacucho, 1977], 32), but this does not mean that he believed in superior groups or in racial hatred. Unlike Emerson, who believed in the superiority of the civilizations of the cold regions, Martí denied the very existence of races. In 1888 Martí wrote, "It is not true . . . that climates influence men enough to twist or alter the essence of their nature, mentally and physically. Because once they are used to it, men grow as variously and as freely in glacial and torrid conditions, with tall people and short, bad and good, obese and slender, tender and coarse" (XI, 480).

41. Lucio V. Mansilla, *Entre—Nos. Causeries del Jueves* (Buenos Aires: Hachette, 1963), 200.

42. On Martí's roots, see Angel Estrada, *La modernidad literaria: De Bécquer a Martí* (Granada: Impredisur, 1992).

43. Martí never advocated forgetting inheritances or ignoring the cultures of other countries; on the contrary, this prologue already shows the precursors to his thesis that one must be knowledgeable in order to choose what is useful, and to liberate oneself from tyrannies, one of the central threads of *Nuestra América* (1889). The contribution of past generations is best expressed in *Ismaelillo*, in the verses "I am my son's son! He recreates me!" Temporality is an essential parameter: Martí is in the past and the future at once, uniting that flow in a constant recreation, condensing rigid oppositions in a mobile and positive image.

44. According to Lionel Gossman, romantic historians considered themselves similar to the heroes of their texts: like them, they participated in the energy of their time and contributed to changing and elaborating it, elevating it by articulating a vision of historical destiny. In "History as Decipherment: Romantic Historiography and the Discovery of the Other" (ms. 44, Princeton University, n.d.)

45. We must not forget that *fin de siècle* society was fertile ground for the resurgence of certain mysticisms, in some cases even occult and esoteric varieties. On the recovery of Christ as an image of the idealist in direct and polemical relation to the

world he inhabits, see the study by Hans Hinterhauser, *Fin de siglo: Figuras y mitos*, trans. María Teresa Martínez (Madrid: Taurus, 1977).

46. Cited by Hinterhauser (36). The effects of this new awareness of temporality are many: writers on both continents rediscovered the pre-Raphaelite woman (wife or mother, nostalgic of a past virginity) as an idealized alternative to both the naturalists' overdeterminined female figures and the "femme fatale" of material opulence. Martí's imagery redeems the woman as mother, but modernists such as Darío and Silva verbalized the drama of desiring either a pure woman or a female satyr. Another point of intersection is the recreation of hybrid mythological beings that reunite dualities, such as the centaur.

47. I am using the parameters set by P. N. Medvedev/M. M. Bakhtin in *The Formal Method in Literary Scholarship: A Critical Introduction to Sociological Poetics*, trans. Albert J. Wehrle (Baltimore: Johns Hopkins University Press, 1978), 129–35. For him genre is the great conditioner of each system of representation: "Genre is the typical form of the whole work, the whole utterance . . . Each element's constructive meaning can only be understood in connection with a genre" (129). The conditioners have an external orientation. They are shaped by the medium in which they are represented, such as a theater or a book, for example, and by the position they have in daily life, institutionalized values, and in general, the discursive practice of a time. The author-reader and internal relationships determine them, as well as the theme as a socio-historical act. They choose to represent a section of reality and have certain media to conceptualize it. The location of the enunciating subject is important, as are textual devices and the type of construction. These parameters, which are so useful as study tools, are not constituted in a rigid mold for the author, who always introduces variants, such as the police novel, satirical poetry, fantastic stories, etc. "The artist must learn to see reality with the eyes of the genre" (134).

Medvedev/Bakhtin's theory, although it is scarcely elaborated, advances the idea that any poetics of genre is also a sociology of the genre, since it reflects not only an author but a collective orientation toward conceptualizing reality. Each innovation is tied to a change in the ways of understanding or in the perception of new aspects of reality. In the case of the modernist chronicles and in relation to that time, this becomes more and more evident. See chapter 3.

48. Edward Said claims that "the best way to consider originality is not to look for the first instances of a phenomenon, but rather to see duplication, parallelism, symmetry, parody, repetition, echoes of it—the way, for example, literature has made itself into a topos of writing" ("On Originality," in *The World, the Text, and the Critic* [Cambridge, Mass.: Harvard University Press, 1983], 135). This is what has been done in this chapter.

49. The museum is a concrete system of ordering an epistemology, an institution that organizes a determined conception of the world based on a selection of heterogeneities. The museum can be academic, but, submitted to subjectivism, is rearticulated in the nonrationality of fantasy. The "I" orders in its own way, and, furthermore,

thematizes in the text the work of quotations: writers have always built a version of the "museum" with their work, of the past, of literary memory. The modernists expose the game, showing the book of Culture and the construction of a new past. Their muse is also in the museum, in the history of literature to which they have chosen to correspond. This is the double play of artifice, because Nature acquires meaning only from the cultural frame, the interpretation of the ordering "I." Although my reasoning does not coincide with theirs in every point, similar ideas can be found in the works previously published by González-Pérez (chapter 1) and by Julio Ramos (chapter 3).

50. I resort to this definition because I consider it more adequate than what can be extracted from Tinianov's analyses. These consider the new as a substitution of systems, or an almost Darwinian evolution, as if each new system were a kind of more advanced child of a preceding system. It is described as a "literary evolution," whereas Castoriardis simply verifies that the new does not imitate, that its essence consists of opening new modes of perceiving reality. This occurs by relating differently already existent elements. To create is to make thinkable what seemed unthinkable (19–23). The tools that Tinianov contributes equally confirm the novelty of the system of representation. The treatment of the modernist image is a literary fact: it has changed the quality of a "function" within the Latin American system of representation. That element is enough to demonstrate the differential quality of the representation with respect to tradition and time, even considering all the internal variants between romanticism on one side, and *costumbrismo*, naturalism, and realism on the other (there are also contemporaneous regionalist forms, such as indigenism and "gauchesca"). See Y. Tinianov, "De la evolución literaria," *Formalismo y vanguardia* (1), trans. Agustín García Tirado (Madrid: Comunicación, Serie B, no. 3, 1973), 115–39.

5. The Years in North America

1. Julio Ramos's *Paradojas de la letra* (Caracas: Ex-cultura, 1996) provides a very intelligent study of Martí, including an excellent analysis of this poem and the theme of exile.
2. Homi K. Bhabha, "The Other Question—the Stereotype and Colonial Discourse," *Screen* 24–26 (Nov.–Dec. 1983): 18–36.
3. "The possibility of formal equality before the law, according to official state ideology, requires uniformity of language and culture among all members of the national community" (Renato Rosaldo, "Social Justice and the Crisis of National Communities," in *Colonial Discourse/Postcolonial Theory*, ed. Francis Barkers, Peter Hulme, Margaret Iverson [Manchester: Manchester University Press, 1994], 239). See also Bill Ashcroft, Gareth Griffiths, and Helen Tiffin, *The Empire Writes Back: Theory and Practice in Post-Colonial Literatures* (London and New York: Routledge, 1989).

4. In his texts the Other can be the United States, presented to the Spanish American "us" as a reality different from their own. But the Other could also be, in Martí's texts as well as Emerson's, those who do not want to see with their own eyes: herd beings, those who are pliable and let themselves be molded by tailors, cobblers, hat makers, pompous and hollow speakers with no pain of their own, scoundrels of common pleasures, and mediocre people who love power and money. The Other is also sometimes, as in the Spanish American literary tradition, the poor and working masses. Lionel Gossman notes that the notion of otherness was the Achilles' heel or point of imbalance of romantic historiography: the fear that their ordered and continuous patterns of historical representation would be broken by the discontinuity of life itself (Lionel Gossman, "History as Decipherment: Romantic Historiography and the Discovery of the Other," *New Literary History* 18 [Autumn 1986]: 23–57). There was something occult and unmanageable that could make history lose its meaning; that hidden threat, therefore, was also the enemy of a rationalized representation of the present: the threat is Sarmiento's barbarism, it is the Other, the marginal, the excluded.

5. Gaston Bachelard, *The Poetics of Space*, trans. M. Jolan (Boston: Beacon Press, 1969).

6. All the quotations from "Grand Livestock Exhibition" are from the anthology José Martí, *Crónicas*, ed. Susana Rotker (Madrid: Alianza, 1993), 196. The same edition has been used for "Coney Island."

7. To understand the American intellectuals' reaction to the Chicago anarchists' proceedings in the New York press, see Thomas Bender's history, especially chapter 5, in *New York Intellect: A History of Intellectual Life in New York City, from 1780 to the Beginnings of Our Own Time* (Baltimore: Johns Hopkins University Press, 1987). For the intellectual field, see Robert E. Spiller et al., *Literary History of the United States*, vol. 2 (New York: Macmillan, 1948), 789–939.

8. Marcelino Menéndez Pelayo, *Historia de los heterodoxos españoles*, vol 7 (Buenos Aires: Espasa-Calpe, 1951), 370. He explains on the same page that in Castelar's prose is a "hidden law of all that monstrous efflorescence, and what gives him a certain blinding and apparent grandness, is nothing more than a big and frightful sophism of one of the greatest of modern sophists."

9. In literature creation is violence and solitude. Roland Barthes theorizes in *Writing Degree Zero* that the writer is always faced with a challenging Form-Object that he wants to possess and destroy, but cannot do so without destroying himself. The Form-Object is tantalizing and impossible, and banishes the writer to solitude (14). *Writing Degree Zero*, introd. Susan Sontag, trans. Annette Lavers and Colin Smith (New York: Hill and Wang, 1968).

10. See A. Trachtenberg, *Brooklyn Bridge: Fact and Symbol* (Chicago: University of Chicago Press, 1977).

11. Jean Starobinski, "1789 et le langage des principes," *Preuves*, no. 203 (January 1968): 22.

12. The *New York Times* (April 28, 1882): 1–2.

13. Michel Pécheux, *Language, Semantics, and Ideology*, trans. Harbans Nagpal (New York: St. Martin's Press, 1982).

14. English cannot replicate Martí's striking use of the adjective *desalados* to describe the men of Charleston. *Desalado* is the past participle of the verb *desalar*, which means both "to remove the wings" and "to be or move about with wings extended."

15. Instead of references to volume and page of the *Obras completas*, I will cite in this chapter my edition of José Martí, *Crónicas*.

16. Judith Butler, *Bodies That Matter: On the Discursive Limits of "Sex"* (New York and London: Routledge, 1993).

17. Henri Lefebvre, *The Production of Space*, trans. Donald Nicholson-Smith (Oxford: Basil Blackwell, 1991), 28.

18. Alfred Fouillé, *Libertad y determinismo*, trans. Luis Alcalá-Zamora y Castillo (Buenos Aires: Atalaya, 1947), 377.

Index

Advertisements, 35, 122n.11
Aguilera, Francisco V., 52
Alberdi, Juan Bautista, 25, 31, 48, 112n.10
Aldrey, Fausto Teodoro de, 35, 37, 38, 46, 101
"Almas Huérfanas, Las" (Gutiérrez Nájera), 3
Altamirano, Ignacio Manuel, 24, 51
Althusser, Louis, 27
Américas, Las (newspaper), 33
"Amor de ciudad grande" (Martí), 84, 86
Argentina: Buenos Aires, 15; journalism's growth in, 38; literacy in, 38; urbanization in, 2. See also *Nación, La* (newspaper)
Art: "art for art's sake," 20, 21; Dewey on, 46; mimetic representation, 74–76, 103, 106; as nature created by man for Marti, 94; as outside the productive world, 107; pure art, 20–21, 118n.20; as re-creating life, 74; social function of, 19–20. *See also* Literature
Artepurismo, 20–21, 118n.20
Associated Press, 63
Avellaneda, Nicolás, 32

Bachelard, Gaston, 85
Bakhtin, M. M., 133n.47
Baltimore Sun (newspaper), 98
Balzac, Honoré de, 46
Barthes, Roland, 12, 44, 108, 135n.9
Baudelaire, Charles, 13, 20, 26, 27
Beauty: democratization of, 61; Martí on, 67; modernist search for ontological, 8; modernists on contemplation of, 21; Rodó on, 19
Beecher, Henry Ward, 67
Bello, Andrés, 29
Benjamin, Walter, 22, 41, 44, 45 Bentham, Jeremy, 7
Berman, Marshall, 12
Bhabha, Homi, 84
Bloom, Harold, 79

Bochet-Huré, Claude, 74
Borges, Jorge Luis, 65, 127n.10
Bourgeoisie: constructivist liberal discourse of, 4; imported goods desired by, 2; modernism and the interiority of, 22, 27; modernism serving the interests of, 26–29, 45; utilitarianism or, 7
Brooklyn Bridge, 82, 88–93, 94–95, 96
Bueno, Manuel, 44
Buenos Aires, 15. *See also* Argentina
Bürger, Peter, 112n.23
Butler, Judith, 100

Caballero, Claudio, 34
"Calasero, El" (Triay), 51
Calderón de la Barca, Pedro, 70
Cambaceres, Eugenio, 24
Campo, Angel de, 51–52
Cané, Miguel, 24
Caracas, 2
"Carta a Bartolomé Mitre y Vedia" (Martí), 86
Casal, Julián del: confessional writing of, 26; on journalism, 39, 43; "Nihilism," 3; occupational range of, 18; social background of, 111n.6
Castelar, Emilio, 37, 56–57, 88, 122n.8, 135n.8
Castoriardis, Cornelius, 83, 134n.50
Castro Leal, Antonio, 38
Catholicism, 118n.25
Censorship, 37
"Centenario americano, El" (Martí), 101, 103
"Centenario de Calderón, El" (Martí), 70
Chadwick, John J., 90
Charleston earthquake, 36, 77, 79, 97, 98–99, 101. *See also* "Terremoto de Charleston, El"
Chicago anarchists, 77, 99–100, 103, 131n.31
Chile, 2
Christ, Martí's images of, 81–82

Chronicles: as break with traditional writing system, 106–7; *Chronique,* 47, 48, 125n.45; as easy to read and attractive to readers, 38; epistemological fissure revealed by, 61; as a genre, 57–59, 82–83; as hybrid, 105, 109; as intermediate between literature and journalism, 36, 59, 106; journalism contrasted with, 105–6; as laboratory of the modernist style, 40; as literature under pressure, 43; as permanent testing laboratory, 109; as poetic, 58–59, 107; poeticization of the real in, 107; precursors of, 47–48; rediscovery of, 105; resistance to discovering full scope of, 45–46; subjectivism of, 105, 108–9

Chronotope, 59

Cities, 15–16; as fragmented for the modernists, 49; growth in late-nineteenth-century, 2; Martí's ambivalence about urban life, 3–4; modernist imagery and lifestyles of, 25; urbanization, 2, 15, 17, 62; urban society revolving around money and practicality, 19

Clichés, 29, 107–8

Colonialism, 84, 95–96

"Coloquio de los centauros" (Darío), 13–14, 22

Commerce, international, 3, 15

"Como se crea un pueblo nuevo en los Estados Unidos" (Martí), 102, 103–4

Comte, Auguste, 5

Conceptualism, 70, 86

"Coney Island" (Martí), 60, 86, 96

"Congreso de Washington, El" (Martí), 97

Cooper, Peter, 67, 68

Coronado, Vicente, 35

Correspondences (Swedenborgian), 13, 78

Costumbrista sketches, 48–52; as not critical of dominant institutions, 52; oratory used in, 65; serialized in newspapers, 34

Crandall, Prudence, 95

Criollismo, 24

Cuba: external issues of, 4; Martí's commitment to liberation of, 127n.1; as remaining under Spanish hegemony, 1

Cultural revolution, 27

Dana, Charles, 62–63, 126n.56

Darío, Rubén: apathy in work of, 3; on clichés, 29, 107–8; "Coloquio de los centauros," 13–14, 22; "Dilucidaciones," 9; "Lo fatal," 3; on form, 21; on his isolation, 20; on Ibsen, 58; impoverished background of, 111n.6; on journalism and style, 39, 43; on journalism's influence on his style, 39–40; on Martí's journalism, 42; on modernism and modernity, 1; newspaper articles of, 36, 122n.12; "not knowing where we're going" in work of, 3; occupational range of, 18; political themes in, 17; *Prosas profanas,* 21; on publishing poetry as difficult, 23; on the pure woman, 133n.46; *Los raros,* 36, 58; on the symbol, 13–14; on the writer as creating a private space, 22; writing for *La Nación,* 37

"Darwin y el Talmud" (Martí), 104

Davidson, Ned, 78–79

Dewey, John, 46

Díaz, Porfirio, 53

Díaz Rodríguez, Manuel, 17

"Dilucidaciones" (Darío), 9

Dis-identification, 96

Doubt, era of, 12

Duality, 69, 83

Dussel, Enrique, 113n.24

Echeverría, Esteban, 78

Edad, de Oro, La (Martí), 97

Editorials, 34

"Emerson" (Martí), 88, 96

Emerson, Ralph Waldo: Mansilla on, 80; Martí on, 59, 67, 68, 69, 73, 75, 93–94; the *New York Times* on, 93–94; and philology, 70, 71; racism of, 132n.40; Spanish American modernists influenced by, 20; on the United States as a utopia, 129n.15

Endecasílabo, 71

Escenas norteamericanas (Martí): expressionist images in, 77; the gaze inverted in, 84, 102–4; gesture of relocation in, 104; on a new kind of literature, 113n.20; as product and agent, 84; scrutiny and admiration in, 67

Estrada, Santiago, 40
Evening Sun (newspaper), 63
Evolution, 2
Exile, 85, 100
Expressionism, 76–77, 106

Fait divers, 47
"Fatal, Lo" (Dario), 3
Femme fatale, 133n.46
Figaro, Le (newspaper), 47, 48, 128n.11
Flaubert, Gustave, 20
Form, poetic, 21
Formalism, 20
Foucault, Michel, 8, 9, 27, 124n.44
Fouillé, Alfred, 66, 67, 104, 128n.115
"Fray Juan sin miedo" (Palma), 49–50
Fuerzas extrañas, Las (Lugones), 33
"Funeral chino, Un" (Martí), 52–53
"Fusilamiento, El" (Campo), 52

Gallas, Helga, 120n.48
Gamboa, Federico, 24
García Marruz, Fina, 10, 45, 62, 130n.22
García Merou, Martín, 19
García Moreno, Alejo, 117n.19
Garfield, James, 69, 76
Gauchesca, 119n.31
Gaze, the, 84–85, 95, 101, 102–4
"Goajiros, Los" (Quintín Suzarte), 50–51
Góngora, Luis de, 70
González, Aníbal, 63, 114n.32
González, Joaquín V., 43
González, Manuel Pedro, 130n.21
González Echevarría, Roberto, 111n.2
González Prada, Manuel, 18, 43, 44, 74
Gossman, Lionel, 132n.44, 135n.4
Gracián, Baltasar, 70
"Grandes huelgas en Estados Unidos, Las" (Martí), 60
"Grand Livestock Exhibition" (Martí), 86
Grant, Ulysses S., 67, 97
"Grito, El" (Prieto), 51
Groussac, Paul, 33, 40, 42
Guerra gaucha, La (Lugones), 24
Gutiérrez, Eduardo, 24
Gutiérrez, Juan María, 32
Gutiérrez Girardot, Rafael, 7, 27, 118n.20
Gutiérrez Nájera, Manuel: "Las Almas Hu-

érfanas," 3; on art as imitation, 75; on beauty, 21; in founding of the chronicle in Spanish America, 47, 48; on a language to express modernity, 104; and modernist syncretism, 13; newspaper articles of, 36; in Spanish American literary rebirth, 124n.41; on telegrams, 33
Guyau, Jean-Marie, 66
Guzmán Blanco, Antonio, 35

Habermas, Jürgen, 11, 16, 17–18, 19, 32
Hegel, Georg Wilhelm Friedrich, 8
Henríquez Ureña, Pedro, 17, 26
Herald (newspaper), 62
Hernández, José, 24
Hernández Arregui, Juan José, 27
Herrera y Reissig, Julio, 18, 111n.6
Highet, Gilbert, 7
Historical fiction, 24
Historicity, 8
Hostos, Eugenio María de, 52
Hour (newspaper), 62
Howells, William Dean, 103
Hyperbaton, 71

Idealism, 81, 82, 103, 108
Identity: dis-identification, 96; language and, 85–88; Martí in search of a shared, 100–101
Ideology, 26–27
Immediacy, 64, 104
Impressionism, 66, 72, 106, 124n.41
Indigenist literature, 119n.31
Industrialization, 1, 2, 15
Intellectual property, 46
International commerce, 3, 15
Internationalism, 25, 33, 34
Introspection, 64–65
"Invasión yankee, La" (Prieto), 51
Ismaelillo (Martí), 3, 64, 132n.43

Jakobson, Roman, 126n.60
Jameson, Fredric, 26, 27
"Jesse James, gran bandido" (Martí), 36, 87–88
Jitrik, Noé, 10, 112n.11
Journalism: advertisements, 35, 122n.11; in Argentina, 38; Associated Press, 63;

Journalism (*continued*)
chronicles contrasted with, 105–6; as
commercial, 32–33; editorials, 34; as
factual, 57; and the flow of the new society, 64; limits of Spanish American,
31–36; versus literature, 36–47; Martí
and the North American press, 62–64;
Martí and the Spanish American press,
52–57; men of letters becoming journalists, 17; modernists and, 28–29, 38–39,
44, 45–46, 108; professionalization of
the journalist, 36–47; telegraphy influ-
encing, 33; temporality of, 43, 61. *See
also* Chronicles; *and organs by name*

Kant, Immanuel, 5, 20, 46
Kaplan, Marcos, 16, 17
Kobre, Sidney, 127n.5
Krause, Carl Christian Friedrich, 5, 20, 46,
74, 117n. 19

Lacan, Jacques, 27, 85
Laclau, Ernesto, 12–13, 26
Landowners, 4
Language: as agent of communal intelli-
gibility, 85; clichés, 29, 107–8; every
occasion meriting its own, 40; for ex-
pressing modernity, 104; identity and,
85–88; neologisms, 70, 71; philology,
8–9, 10, 70
Larra, Mariano José de, 128n.11
Latifundios, 15 Latin America. *See* Spanish
America
Leenhardt, Jacques, 115n.42
Lefebvre, Henri, 103
Leroux, Pierre, 3, 112n.14
"Leyenda de la ciencia, La" (Castelar), 56,
122n.8
Literacy, 38
Literati, the, 16
Literature: versus journalism, 36–47; literary and political discourses separated,
16–17; logic of literary representation,
10–11; and morality, 19–20; as object
of leisure, 19; originality required in,
46, 107–8; popular genres and authors,
24; professionalization of the writer,
36–47; serialized fiction in newspapers,

33–34; social context of, 108; as voca-
tion in Spanish America, 17–18; writers
as working class, 41; the writers' role,
15–30. *See also* Poetry
Logic of literary representation, 10–11
Longfellow, Henry Wadsworth, 69
Longinus, 67, 129n.15
López, Lucio Vicente, 24
López Portillo, José, 24
Lorenzo-Rivero, Luis, 128n.11
Lugones, Leopoldo, 17, 23–24, 33, 111n.6
Luhman, Nilkas, 115n.39

"Madre América" (Martí), 97
Mañach, Jorge, 2
Mansilla, Lucio V., 80
Marinello, Juan, 25
Martí, José: advertisements written by, 33;
on aesthetics and form, 20–21; ambivalence about urban life, 3–4; on American taste in literature, 44; anti-
academicism of, 29; as baroque, 71,
130nn.21, 22; on Brooklyn Bridge, 82,
88–93, 94–95, 96; Catholicism's influence on, 118n.25; on Charleston earthquake, 36, 77, 79, 97, 98–99, 101; on
Chicago anarchists, 77, 99–100,
131n.31; Christ's image in work of, 81–
82; on compiling his journalistic texts,
36; on contradictions resulting from
modernity, 1–2; on contrasts in Latin
American life, 4–5; on a creative subjectivity united with history, 10; on criticism and synthesis, 14; and Cuban liberation, 127n.1; Darío on journalism of,
42; a definitive religion sought by, 8;
dualistic thinking of, 69; on Emerson,
59, 67, 68, 69, 73, 75, 93–94; expressionism of, 7677; on formalism, 20; in
founding of the chronicle in Spanish
America, 47–48; on human types, 52–
53, 132n.40; idealism of, 82; immediate
witness strategy of, 101–2; impressionism of, 66, 72, 106; on intellectual property, 46; and introspection, 64–65; on
journalism, 38, 39, 40, 45; liberal faith
in progress of, 5; liberal views of, 75;
on local culture's precariousness, 25,

119n.35; on musical effects in writing, 78–79; on Nature, 67, 74–75, 79–80, 97; neologisms of, 70, 71; in North America, 84–104; and the North American press, 62–64; occupational range of, 18; in oratorical tradition, 65–69; on originality, 108; past cultures as influence on, 10; phases of exile of, 96–97; and philology, 9, 70; on realism, 63–64; as a revolutionary, 7; as a romantic, 64, 82; Sarmiento on journalism of, 42; on science versus mystery, 5; "Sección constante" column, 35, 47; on social function of art, 19; in Spanish American literary rebirth, 124n.41; and the Spanish American press, 52–57; on spirit of the new age, 3; on style, 40–41; subjectivism of, 64, 81, 103, 106; symbolism of, 66, 70, 75, 77–78; syncretism of, 13, 79–81; temporality represented by, 60–62, 72, 74, 82; on Whitman, 58, 67, 68, 72–74, 77, 120n.24; writing as artifice for, 74–78; writing as practice opposed to the state for, 18; writing for *La Nación,* 37, 46, 101; writing for *La Opinión Nacional,* 37, 46, 47, 48, 53–54, 101. See also *Escenas norteamericanas;* "Prólogo al Poema del Niágara de Pérez Bonalde"; *and other works by name*

Marx, Karl, 11, 14, 41
Mass culture, 61
Matto de Turner, Clorinda, 24
McLuhan, Marshall, 43
Medvedev, P. N., 133n.47
"Mejor amigo . . . un perro, El" (Palma), 49
Menéndez Pelayo, Marcelino, 56, 135n.8
Mexico City, 15
Mill, John Stuart, 72
Mimesis, 74–76, 103, 106
Mitre, Bartolomé, 37, 46, 59, 87, 101
Modernism: aesthetics replacing faith for, 8; aristocratic inclinations of, 28; bourgeois interests served by, 26–29, 45; bourgeois interiority in, 22, 27; Catholicism's influence on, 118n.25; the chronicle as laboratory of style of, 40; cities as the environment of, 15; class-

less social position of, 4, 23; commercialism rejected by, 20, 21–22; confessional writing of, 26; displacement and vertigo suffered by, 6–7; epistemological rupture experienced by, 8; estrangement as theme of, 12; ideologizing function of, 26–27; imbalance in poetry of, 3; as importing foreign culture, 29–30; internationalism of, 25; and journalism, 28–29, 38–39, 44, 45–46, 108; logic of literary representation of, 10–11; malaise of, 3, 4; and the marginalized elite, 4; and modernity, 1, 11; narrator's position emphasized by, 63; philology as interest of, 8–9, 10; of post-independence literature, 6; and progress, 26; realism contrasted with, 81; and romanticism, 7; on social function of art, 19–20; subjectivism of, 8–10; the suprareal in work of, 28; symbology of, 13; syncretism of, 13; system of narration of, 13; on technique as the essence of writing, 10; texts as semiotic machines, 112n.11; universalization of, 25; "will to style" of, 21
Modernity: and America as the "New World," 6; awareness of as suffusing everything, 64; for late-nineteenth-century Spanish America, 1; Martí on a language to express, 104; modernism's relationship to, 1, 11; the problem of, 1–3; as system of notions, 3
Modernization, 6, 12, 33
Monsiváis, Carlos, 48–49, 52
Morality, art and, 19–20
"Mulata de rumbo, La" (Paula Gelabert), 51
Museums, 133n.49
Musicality, 78–79, 106
Mysticism, 132n.45

Nación, La (newspaper), 32–39; blurred generic boundaries in, 34; foreign correspondents of, 33; Martí asked to moderate his judgments, 46, 101; Martí writing for, 37, 46, 87, 101; *La Opinión Nacional de Caracas* compared with, 34–35, 55–56; and Partido Liberal, 31; serialized fiction in, 33–34

Nación Argentina, La (newspaper), 32
"Narraciones fantásticas" (Martí), 34, 102
Naturalism, 24, 61, 81
Nature, 67, 74–75, 79–80, 97
Neologisms, 70, 71
Newspapers. *See* Journalism
New York City: Martí and the North American press, 62–64; Martí's exile in, 84–104; population growth of, 15; realist-idealist struggle in, 81, 103
New York Times (newspaper), 63, 87, 93–94, 98
New York Tribune (newspaper), 63, 90, 98
Nietzsche, Friedrich, 11
"Nihilism" (Casal), 3
Novels of manners, 24
"Nuestra América" (Martí), 18, 80, 85, 86, 97, 132n.43

Objectivity, 57, 63
Oligarchy, 15
Ong, Walter, 79
Opinión Nacional de Caracas, La (newspaper): advertisements in, 35; on Charleston earthquake, 99; "Hortensio" items, 54–55; internationalism of, 34–35; Martí gives up his post with, 46, 101; Martí's "Sección constante" column, 35, 47; Martí writing for, 37, 47, 48, 53–54; *La Nación* compared with, 34–35, 55–56
Oratory, 65–69 Originality, 46, 80, 107–8, 133n.48
Ortega y Gasset, José, 58
Ortíz, Fernando, 30
Other, the: in Altamirano, 51; in *costumbrista* sketches, 49–50, 52; and the gaze, 84; Martí as, 84; in Martí's texts, 135n.4; the United States as, 85, 100, 103
Oyuela, Calixto, 23, 41

Palma, Ricardo, 47, 49–50
Parnassianism, 20, 46, 61, 66, 72, 78, 124n.41
Paula Gelabert, Francisco de, 50, 51
Payno, Manuel, 24
Paz, Octavio, 7, 11

Peasants, 4
Pêcheux, Michel, 95–96
Pérez Bonalde, Juan Antonio. *See* "Prólogo al Poema del Niágara de Pérez Bonalde" (Martí)
Perús, Françoise, 25, 41, 123n.27
Peruvian Traditions (Palma), 47, 49–50
Phillips, Wendell, 68, 76
Philology, 8–9, 10, 70
Plastic surgery, 35–36
Plato, 67
"Poema del Niágara" (Pérez Bonalde). *See* "Prólogo al Poema del Niágara de Pérez Bonalde" (Martí)
"Poeta Walt Whitman, El," 96
Poetic form, 21
Poeticization of the real, 82, 107
Poetic syncretism, 79–81, 132n.39
Poetry: chronicles as poetic, 58–59, 107; and collapse of traditional beliefs, 62; and musicality, 78–79; in Spanish American culture, 23–24
Portuondo, José Antonio, 21
Positivism, 6, 7, 11, 61, 78
Post-structuralism, 12
Power, 85
Pre-Raphaelites, 133n.46
Press, the. *See* Journalism
Prieto, Guillermo, 51
Progress, 5, 7, 11, 26
Proletariat, 4
"Prólogo al Poema del Niágara de Pérez Bonalde" (Martí): on breaking away from literary convention, 81; on central issue of his time, 8; on democratization of writing, 42; on journalism as the place for ideas, 108; on Nature for the new poets, 74; on philology, 70; on return to conceptualism, 86; temporality represented in, 60–61
Prosas profanas (Darío), 21
"Puente de Brooklyn, El" (Martí), 82, 88–93, 94–95, 96
Puerto Rico, 1, 4
Punctuation, 68, 129n.19
Pure art, 20–21, 118n.20

Quesada, Ernesto, 42

Quintín Suzarte, José, 50–51
Quiroga, Horacio, 33

Races, 80, 132n.40
Rama, Angel: on Darío's newspaper articles, 122n.12; on ideologizing function of modernism, 26; on the malaise of modernism, 4; on Martí and universalism, 130n.20; on modernism and modernity, 1; on modernists having few options, 38–39; on professional specialization of the writer, 18; on Rimbaud, 77, 131n.32; on transculturation, 30; on universalization of the modernists, 25
Ramos, Julio, 90, 92, 114n.26
Raros, Los (Darío), 36, 58
Rationalization, 6–7, 19, 49, 50, 65, 113n.23
Raw materials, 15
Real de Azúa, Carlos, 4, 28
Realism: versus idealism in New York, 81, 103; Martí on, 63–64; modernist chronicle contrasted with, 61; popularity of, 24
Redemption, 82
Regionalism, 71, 80
Reification, 28, 120n.45
Renan, Ernest, 9, 82, 114n.32
Reporters, 33
Residual need, 19
"Responso" (Silva), 21
"Retrato de Francisco V. Aguilera" (Hostos), 52
Revista Cubana (periodical), 128n.13
Revista Venezolana (periodical), 40, 41, 54
Reyes, Carlos, 24
Riis, Jacob, 63
Rimbaud, Arthur, 77, 131n.32
Rodó, José Enrique, 18, 19
Roebling, John A., 90
Rojas, Arístedes, 99
Romanticism: Martí's poetics contrasted with those of, 64, 82; modernism compared with, 7, 9, 20; and philology, 70; on poetry as in the idea, 78; quasi-religious character of, 81; and writers, dissociation from the mainstream, 16

Romero, José Luis, 2, 16, 17, 27
Rosaldo, Renato, 134n.3
"Rostro rehecho, El" (Martí), 35–36
Russell, Bertrand, 12

Said, Edward, 133n.48
Sanín Cano, Baldomero, 72, 75–76
Santos Chocano, José, 17
Sarmiento, Domingo F.: Caballero debate, 34; editorial in *La Nación,* 55–56; on Martí's journalism, 42, 101; modernists contrasted with, 29; in oratorical tradition, 128n.11; on the Other, 50; on poetry as in the idea, 78; on writing and modernization, 6, 50
Schulman, Iván, 124n.41
Science, 5, 8, 9, 11
Secularization, 6, 7–8, 65, 74
Serialized fiction, 33–34
Service economy, 15
"Siete pelos del diablo, Los" (Palma), 50
Silva, José Asunción: occupational range of, 18; political themes in, 17; on practical reality, 20; on the pure woman, 133n.46; "Responso," 21; *Sobremesa,* 20; social background of, 111n.6; on verse as sacred, 21
Sobremesa (Silva), 20
Solipsism, 9
Sombart, Werner, 31
Space of condensation, 10, 12–14, 26, 81, 82, 108
Spanish America: journalism in, 31–36; literature as vocation in, 17–18; Martí and the press of, 52–57; *mestizo* condition of, 80; modernity in, 1–5; poetry in culture of, 23–24; rationalizing spirit of post-independence literature, 6; as raw materials source, 15–16; urbanization in, 2, 15
Starobinski, J., 92
Stedman, Edmund Clarence, 103
Structuralism, 82, 126n.1 subjectivism, 8–10; of chronicles, 105, 108–9; of Martí, 64, 81, 103, 106; and the museum, 133n.49; versus rationalization in modernity, 7; of Rimbaud, 77; solipsism, 9
Sublime, Martí's oratorical strategies for representing the, 65–69

Sun (newspaper), 62–63, 87, 91, 92–93, 97, 127n.5
Suspicion, era of, 7, 10–12
Swedenborg, Emmanuel, 13, 78
Symbolism: of Christ in Martí's work, 81–82; equivocal discourse of, 116n.47; and generalized doubt, 72; of Martí, 66, 70, 75, 77–78; of the modernists, 21; as system of narration, 13–14
Syncretism, poetic, 79–81, 132n.39
Synesthesia, 13, 66, 77

Tablada, Juan José, 17
Tableau vivant, 50
Tarde, Gabriel, 66
Telegraph, 33
Temporality, 43, 60–62, 72, 74, 82, 126n.1
"Terremoto de Charleston, El" (Martí), 36, 77, 79, 97, 98–99, 101. *See also* Charleston earthquake
Tinianov, Y., 134n.50
Transculturation, 30, 79
Transparency, illusion of, 103
Triay, José E., 50, 51
Twain, Mark, 63

Unamuno, Miguel de, 66
Universalism, 71, 80, 130n.20
Urbanization, 2, 15, 17, 62
Uruguay, 2
Utilitarianism, 5, 7, 21

Valencia, Guillermo, 17

Valera, Juan, 124n.31
Valerio, Francisco, 50, 51
Varona, Enrique José, 65–66
Véliz, Claudio, 2, 15, 17
Venezuela: Caracas, 2; *Revista Venezolana,* 40, 41, 54; urbanization in, 2. See also *Opinión Nacional de Caracas, La* (newspaper)
Verisimilitude, 57–58, 86
Verlaine, Paul, 78
Versos libres (Martí), 3, 71
Versos sencillos (Martí), 80
Viana, Javier de, 24
Villemont, Auguste, 125n.45
"Visita a la Candelaria de los Patos, Una" (Altamirano), 51
Vitier, Cintio, 130n.22

Weber, Max, 6, 12
Whitman, Walt: Borges on, 127n.10; Martí on, 58, 67, 68, 72–74, 77, 120n.24; Martí reading, 63; Martí's "El poeta Walt Whitman," 96; Martí's oratory compared with that of, 66; on the United States as utopian, 129n.15
Wilde, Eduardo, 19
Williams, Raymond, 57, 108
Woman, 133n.46
Writing. *See* Literature

"¡Zacatecas!" (Valerio), 51
Zeno Gandía, Manuel, 24
Zola, Émile, 75, 81, 103